Grandma, Can We Talk?

Tips for Grampa and Grandma Getting Along With the Grandkids

By Dr. Roger McIntire

Copyright © 2017 Summit Crossroads Press

Summit Crossroads Press
9329 Angelina Circle
Columbia, MD 21045
1-410-290-7058
E-mail: SumCross@aol.com
http://www.parentsuccess.com

Multiple copies of Dr. McIntire's books may be purchased at discount from the publisher.

ISBN No. 978-0-9991565-0-6

LCCN No. 2017912704

All rights reserved. No part of the material protected by this copyright notice may be reproduced or utilized in any form or by any means, electronic or mechanical, including photocopying, recording, or by information storage and retrieval system without written permission from the publisher. Printed in the United States of America.

About the Author

Dr. Roger McIntire, father of three, grampa of two, taught child and adolescent psychology, behavior analysis and family counseling at the University of Maryland for 32 years. He has authored eight books including *Teenagers and Parents: 12 Steps to a Better Relationship, Staying Cool and In Control, Enjoy Successful Parenting*, and *For Love of Children*.

In addition to working with families, he consulted with teachers in preschools, grade schools, high schools and colleges. Dr. McIntire's research publications (over 100) have dealt with infant vocalizations, eating problems, strategies in school teaching, high school motivation and reasons for college drop-outs.

4 - Dr. Roger McIntire

Table of Contents

Preface - 9

Suggestion 1: Listen Well - What's your favorite topic? - 13

1. "What Are You Saying About Me?" - 13
2. Slow Down, Use "It" Not "You" - 17
3. Careful When Teaching Lessons and Fixing Blame - 20
4. Looking, Smiling and Other "Non-Verbal" Signals - 23
5. Pass Up the "Quick Fix" - 26
6. The Real Topic May Not Have Come Up Yet - 27
7. Suggest Solutions with Care - 32
8. Beware of Arguments for Entertainment - 35

Suggestion 2: Avoid the Shortcuts- *Give* a nice day. -39

1. One-ups and Put-downs Are, Too often, a Part of Shortcut Grandparenting - 42
2. Who Deserves the Blame, or the Credit? - 53
3. Look for Needs Instead of Blames - 58

4. Avoid the Temptation to Increase Blame as They Grow Up - 60
5. "I Always Felt I was Never Good Enough" - 62

Suggestion 3: Watch Out For The Games - Every time we win we make a loser - 65
1. What Games? - 65
2. Listening During the Game - 73
3. Watch for a Chance to Encourage Something Better - 74
4. Use Careful Messages for Grandsons and Daughters - 75
5. Encourage Enjoyment of Success - 80

Suggestion 4: Careful With Punishment, It Has Great Disadvantages - You can't make a garden just by pulling weeds - 85
1. Ten Reasons "Get Tough" Advice from Tough Grampa is Off Track - 86
2. Negative Reinforcement - 99
3. Why Would Anyone Use Punishment? - 107
4. Five Alternatives to Punishment - 108

Suggestion 5: Help with the "Boy Problem" and School Work - For every 100 male college graduates

there are 140 women graduates. - 125
1. The "Boy Problem" - 125
2. Who is Gifted? - 129
3. Bullies and Victims Hiding Out in School - 132
4. Magical and Mental Habits - 137

Suggestion 6: Helping Your Grandchild Make Friends - How can you say, "I Like You"? - 145
1. How Do You Like Your Grandchildren? - 146
2. "Likable" is More than Asking Questions - 147
3. Liking and Caring Behaviors are Attractive - 152
4. The Media Can Help Communication About Social Skills - 154
5. Talking About Sex - 156
6. Set Priorities, Raise Questions and Listen - 162
7. A Disposition Creates Its Own Surroundings - 171
8. Children, Parents and Grandparents Learn Each Other's Habits 174

Suggestion 7: The Bad Habits of Alcohol, Drugs, and Cars - "I figure, you know, what do I have to lose?" - 177
1. Is Alcohol the Most Dangerous Substance? - 177
2. Don't Send the Wrong Messages - 178
3. Drugs and Self-Esteem - 182

4. Medications: " I Didn't Get My Pill Today, Can I Help It? - 184
5. Drugs and Other Troubles After School - 191
6. Checklists for Habits and Behavior - 196
7. Depression - 199
8. Smoking - 202
9. The Battle of the Bulge - 206
10. Cars and the Driving Threat - 208
11. College is Coming, Why Some Quit and Others Stay the Course - 211

Suggestion 8: About Social Media - Chatting with friends online is not a waste, but 800.000 sex offenders are online, too! - 217
1. Computer Companions - 217
2. Do They Have an Electronic Addiction? - 222
3. The Dangers of Social Media - 223
4. Friends, Bullies and Meanies All Chime In on the Net - 224
5. The Consequences of Being Busted! - 227

The Last Word: Graduation - 231

Preface

Most grandparents hope to reach across the generation gap to communicate and possibly help their grandchildren. But our "techno-obsessed" children often don't see much beyond their little electric windows and may have no appreciation for any story with roots before 2000.

Nevertheless, communication styles--online, by phone or in person--can build a grandson's or daughter's enjoyment and comfort with Grandma's and Grampa's attempts to talk with them. The first four chapters of this book focus on this topic: How to do the talking.

All the other topics in this book will be easier if the talking is comfortable for you <u>and</u> your grandchild.

Grandparents are more important in the lives of children than they were in past generations. Free time for parenting has become a scarce commodity, and often both Dad and Mom have fulltime jobs that are part of the competition. More of their time is given to commuting, TV, and family responsibilities. Often, computers also take up family time. Most of whatever scraps of time are left go to child-rearing. We are certainly in an era of time poverty.

Grandparents may have a little more freedom to spend time with the kids. If they do, it is all the more precious in these high-tech times. Leisurely, unstressed conversation with the kids may become almost entirely "grandparent time."

Grandparents are special. They can provide a safe place for talk about subjects Mom and Dad may find uncomfortable or too complicated for the time available.

Even the toddlers have a desire to break free from parental control. Fortunately, it is mixed with a desire for admiration and support from both parents and grandparents. Of course, teenagers want to be on their own and different from the adult generations they are leaving behind. And conversely, parents and grandparents want their children to stay close to their example and be more like them.

Childhood is partly a struggle to win greater independence. Parenting is partly a struggle to properly decrease control. Grandparenting is partly a task to help with both struggles.

Even before our grandchildren reach ten, they're starting to grow into teenagers. Their temptations multiply and everything becomes faster, more dangerous, and harder to evaluate. Sex, drugs, and cars become part of the adolescent years surprisingly early. To keep up, grandparents must listen a lot.

All of the theories—about siblings, birth order, genetics and early experiences—contribute understanding, but such past influences cannot be changed. Grandma's and Grampa's best opportunity to influence what is going on, really their only opportunity, is confined to the here-and-now.

12 - Dr. Roger McIntire

Suggestion 1: Listen Well

What's your favorite topic?

When your grandchild asks, *"Grandma (or Grampa), can we talk?"* your answer needs to be a careful one. If you have this part right, your adult experience will be available to your grandkids at a low price. Go slowly here and review your conversational habits when talking with your grandchildren.

1. "What are You Saying About Me?"

Your pet dog will perk up his ears whenever his name is mentioned. Most children beyond the toddler stage have the same interest. They "tune in" to the parts of conversations that are about them, and they are a little less interested in the rest. The most important part of the conversation will be, *"What are you saying about me?"* Talks with grandchildren can go sour immediately when we think their *mistakes* are the most important topics, while the children, first of all, pay attention to the implied *personal evaluation*!

"You should have seen what happened in school today, Grandma."

"What, Donald?"

"Keith got in an argument with Mr. Effort, and they ended up in a real fight!"

"I'm sure it wasn't much of a fight."

"Yes, it was. They were wrestling!"

"I hope you didn't have anything to do with it."

"Naw, all I did was cheer."

"Cheer? Listen, Donald, you'll end up in trouble right along with Keith! Don't you have any more sense than to..."

Let's interrupt Grandma here for a moment. She criticized Donald's story: (1) she thinks Donald exaggerated because it wasn't much of a fight, (2) she thinks Donald might have had something to do with it, and (3) she thinks Donald should not have cheered.

Grandma centered the conversation on what she disliked about Donald's behavior instead of the story. All this happened in a 20-second talk. Donald, like most children, will resent the way his Grandma turned his story into a talk about his mistakes. In the future, Donald will drift further away, and Grandma will get fewer chances to talk.

Grandma's style of continual correction puts Donald on the defensive. Donald only wanted to tell his story for the joy of it, without corrections that lead in other directions. Here's the first point of possible misunderstanding and conflict. A child may extract a signal of personal evaluation in less than a sentence. If the signals are negative, up come the defensive reactions before any useful exchange begins.

Let's back up and give Grandma a second chance with Donald's story and see how she can steer clear of making it all about Donald.

"You should have seen what happened in gym today, Grandma."

"What, Donald?"

"Keith got in an argument with Mr. Effort, and they ended up in a real fight!"

"How did it all start?" (Grandma ignores the possible exaggeration, doesn't express doubt, and shows interest instead.)

"They just started arguing about the exercises, and Keith wouldn't give in."

"Hard to win against the teacher." (Grandma's

comment is a general remark about teacher-student relationships, and it's not critical of Donald.)

"Yeah, Keith is in big trouble."

"Did they ever get around to the exercises?" (Grandma is interested in the story, not just in making points and giving advice.)

"Keith was sent to the office, and then we tried these safety belts for the flips. Do you know about those?"

"I don't think we had them in my school."

"Well, they have these ropes..."

Donald may have a clearer view of the incident now, and he may understand the hopelessness of Keith's argumentative attitude. He wasn't distracted by having to defend himself when he told Grandma the story. And now he's explaining something to his Grandmother. Grandma *wants* to hear Donald's story, not give him a lesson about his behavior and possible mistakes.

Children are forever on guard to protect their fragile self-confidence. Donald is on the lookout for Grandma's opinion of him. We grandparents sometimes concentrate our efforts on their childish mistakes, but the kids give the lessons a low rating, at best.

2. Slow Down, Use "It" Not "You."

Deliberately slow your pace of conversation so your child-teen can slow his. Even a sassy teenager is not likely to have your way with building thoughts into words and will become defensive when he's rushed or runs out of vocabulary.

Ten-year-old Marie: *"This terrorism business is awful."*

Grandma: *"Well, you just have to learn to live with it. The world is dangerous."*

An argument has already started. Of course, Grandma didn't mean that terrorism is not awful, she just moved on (too quickly) and made Marie the topic instead of terrorism (You just have to learn…) and missed her opportunity to agree with her granddaughter.

Grandma is next in line for a "Yes, but…," an exchange leading to a louder argument because her pace is too fast. Now the focus has changed to Marie winning the argument. Grandma will make her points, and Marie will struggle to stay even. Distracted now by the argument, there will be little help with anxieties about terrorism. Grandkids in this situation copy the adult's argumentative style of looking for mistakes to correct. A simple conversation has turned into a competition.

Eleven-year-old grandson, Joey: *"I've got so much homework."*

Grandma: *"Sounds like…they gave you…a lot."* (Good remark. with a slow pace, and Grandma only repeats what her grandchild said.)

Joey: *"How can I do all of this?"*

Grandma: *"Well, why not start with…"* (Grandma stops and remembers to avoid jumping in with advice.)

Joey: *"I'm not going to do any of it!"*

Grandma starts to remind her grandson he's likely to be grounded for the week if homework is not done, but Grandma remembers to avoid punishment and instead says, *"You're really good at math, maybe you could start there."* (Grandma risks a quick-fix mistake, but mixed with the compliment about math, it's likely to be taken positively.)

Learning the "it-habit" instead of the "you-habit" can also reduce the stress of conversation by allowing her youngster to stay on his topic. When Grandma got her second chance with Donald, she said, *"How did it all start?"* Using "it" helped avoid the instant-evaluation-of-Donald pitfall, it also helps Grandma avoid taking over the topic.

When a conversation seems threatening to your grandson or daughter, keep your conversation slow and look at the subject as an "it" instead of "you." This tactic avoids the trap of "attack, defense, counter-attack, and counter-defense." Conversation doesn't make a good competitive sport.

Let's give Grampa a chance.

Grampa: *Leave your baby brother alone, Justin.*

Five-year-old Justin: *I was just going to pat him.*

Grampa's first impulse may be to say, "*I know what you were going to do, just stay away, you'll wake him!*" His second impulse might be, "*I like to pat him, too. But it might wake him, and he's tired.*"

Justin drops some crumbs from his potato chip bag.

Now Grampa's first impulse might be to say, "*You are so messy! Look what you did!*"

But his second impulse might be, "*Oh, look what happened. Better pick those up before they get trampled into the carpet.*"

If Grampa chooses his first impulse in these examples, he emphasizes Justin, the person. *You* will wake him, *you* are messy. If he chooses his second reaction to each event, he emphasizes a situation *he and Justin* are dealing with together: *It* will wake him. Look *what* happened. It won't make a lot of difference to Justin on these two occasions. But over the long haul, Justin will end up with a very different message about himself and a very different relationship with Grampa.

3. Careful When Teaching Lessons and Fixing Blame.

The opportunities to "teach a lesson" and "fix the blame" are temptations most of us grandparents find hard to resist. But sometimes the benefit of getting more facts outweighs the "quick-fix" or the "make-them-sit-up-and-take-notice" approach. People who avoid instant evaluation and defuse confrontation with an objective conversation of "it" topics are easier to talk to. They are interested in the other person's experiences not in placing blame or emphasizing mistakes.

Grandma: *"How was art class today?"*
Eight-year-old, Amy: *"OK, what I saw of it."*
Grandma: *"What do you mean?"*
Amy: *"Mrs. Clay sent me to the office."*
Grandma: *"What did you do?"* (Attack #1)
Amy: *"I didn't do anything!"* (Defense)
Grandma: *"You must have done something; you*

aren't sent to the office for nothing!" (Attack #2, conversation going badly)

Amy: *"You never think it's the teacher's fault; you always blame me."* (Counter-attack, looking for a way out)

Grandma: *"What kind of talk is that? Let's have the whole story."* (Attack #3, conversation almost destroyed.)

Amy: *"Oh, nuts!"* Amy stomps out. (Conversation dead.)

Grandma can do better by avoiding the personal evaluation and using the "it' for topics instead.

Grandma: *"How was art class today?"*

Amy: *"Oh, OK, what I saw of it."*

Grandma: *"What do you mean?"*

Amy: *"Mrs. Clay sent me to the office."*

Grandma: *"WHAT happened?"* (Emphasizes "it" instead of Amy). IT happened. This is much better than, "What did you do?")

Amy: *"Tom ripped my paper."* (The conversation takes a new turn with Amy's answer to the "it" question.)

Grandma: *"Oh, no!"* (Emphasizes sympathy rather than an evaluation of the upcoming mistake.)

Amy: *"Yeah, so I shoved him."*

Grandma: *"And so she sent you to the office?"* (Grandma's focus is on facts and sympathy instead of taking advantage of a chance to reprimand something that's already been reprimanded at school.)

Amy: *"Yeah."*

Grandma: *"Then what happened?"* (Good "it" question. It avoids "let's get to the bottom of [your mistake in] this!")

Amy: *"Well, for one thing, I'm behind in art again."*

Grandma: *"Well, if you can stay away from Tom, maybe you'll catch up. What else happened today?"* (Grandma adds a little parental advice and then on to looking for something more positive.)

Too often we grandparents begin at the wrong end of the conversation. After our grandson or daughter exposes a problem or troublesome topic, we often jump to the end in order to fix the problem. In our rush, the message becomes, *"Stop talking; you're wrong, I'm right, and I'll tell you what to do."*

Effective conversational strategies take time, but if they become a habit, the rough parts of family talk can become smoother. A side benefit is the grandkids learn a better way to talk to others.

4. Looking, Smiling and Other "Non-Verbal" Signals.

There is more to conversation than what is said and what is heard. Folding arms, speaking louder, and looking away all say volumes. Looking is particularly important. For example, watching the TV while holding your finger over the mute button ready to restore the sound, may irritate your offspring more than a yawn. A child will quickly learn these signals and may increase his aggressive style just to regain your attention.

Smiling can also be a big factor in getting along. One marriage councilor I know said she counts the expressions of support and agreement between husband and wife. If she notes less than six per hour together, she becomes pessimistic about the relationship. However, she counts smiling as one of the positive expressions. Actually, she counts every smile as two in looking for six per hour.

A slump may also show an uninterested attitude. It's best to sit up and face your conversational partner. To accept your solution your grandson has to stop thinking about himself and take up the courage to admit you could be right. Knowing how seldom he is likely to reach this opinion, smile, sit up, and show interest. Most talks with the grandkids will not reach a conclusion. That's OK, family conversation should not be a tennis game where every ball must be returned, and every game scored and posted. Let it end as it so often does with your friends at work—additional understanding and support, but no answers.

Give a nice day. Practice these habits with another grandparent or a friend while you share a simple story such as getting the kids to school or helping them with homework. Begin with one person as the listener and one as the teller. Review the following guidelines for good listening.

Keep frequent eye contact. Look at your conversation partner most of the time. A child expects a good listener to look at him/her. We don't like to feel unattended because the person we're talking with is staring at the newspaper or TV while we ask a question. Children feel that way too.

Smile at your grandkids frequently. It's a sign you found something good about them. They appreciate it.

Use good posture. Face your grandchild while talking and listening. Use body language that says, *"I'm alert! I'm interested!"* A grandparent who slumps, looks away, or even walks away sends messages that discourage and insult the person talking.

Shy grandchildren might want to leave an awkward situation with a grandparent they don't see often. Asking open-ended questions might keep the conversation comfortable enough.

Avoid criticism; ask questions instead. Use questions that continue the conversation by asking for longer, and hopefully slower, answers instead of just *"yes"* or *"no." "How did it feel?"* is more likely to continue the talk than *"Did you feel bad?"* Emphasize *IT* questions instead of using *YOU*: *"How was it at school today?"* not *"How did you do at school today?"* Careful questions can help in a neutral, non-opinionated way, so the person asking the questions gains a better understanding of what happened and why.

Use reflective statements. Re-word the last thing your grandchild said to show you understand what he/she told you. *"Boy, I really hate Mr. Jones for math!"* could be answered with a response that merely reflects the same idea in different words and it also confirms you got it, *"He really annoys you"* or *"You get mad at him sometimes, I guess."*

Avoid solution statements. Replace the

temptation to give advice or criticize by reflecting your grandchild's statements instead. Suggestions such as *"Why don't you . . .?"* or *"Have you tried . . .?"* might make the storyteller feel inferior, resentful, and argumentative. Your listening helps because the speaker will clarify, for both of you, the situation and his feelings.

Share your experience. Share stories, jokes, and experiences that helped you learn about getting along in life. Be selective, avoid stories that are too close to a sore point with your grandchildren. If they feel your experiences are not directed as advice to their specific weaknesses, the tales can be enjoyed and will improve the relationship.

5. Pass Up the "Quick-Fix."

Parents and grandparents love to fix things, especially quickly! Grandparents, particularly grampas, it seems, can be too efficiency-oriented in their conversations with kids. If you told me you had trouble tying your shoe because the lace broke, would you want me to tell you how to fix it? No. As a matter of fact, it would be a bit insulting because it implies that I think you are a klutz!

Jumping in with a "quick fix" is often annoying

because if Grandma or Grampa jumps in too soon with advice, a child or teen may cancel his or her next topic entirely—just to avoid more correction.

Better to jump in with a positive remark first. Identify and highlight the behaviors you like. Love is not much without liking specific behaviors also. Grandma's and Grampa's first job is to find and compliment what is likable about their grandkids. Even when the grandkids feel obligated to brush them off, compliments will encourage them. Repeat as needed. Learning is a process, not a single event.

6. The Real Topic May Not Have Come Up Yet.

Reactions that repeat what a child just said often result in more information from the child. Her first remarks are usually long on feelings and short on facts. Reflective remarks may encourage her to make up the shortfall. Also, a reflective remark can be satisfying to her because it says you understand.

Don't try to fill every pause; some silence is ok. Don't meet their expectation that you always have advice to give. Slow your pace so you have time to think. If grandparents jump in with early advice or opinions, their reactions could be way off target.

Reflective statements say nothing new and only

repeat what your grandson or granddaughter said in different words. Without adding anything new, this agreement keeps the conversation going and provides opportunities to get straightforward information without defensiveness.

Reflective statements also require a little creativity to avoid looking simple-minded or manipulative, but in small amounts these reactions can allow the kids to continue *their* topic of conversation. Let's look at an example of reflective statements in action by a grandma learning about her granddaughter.

Amy: *"Man, is that school boring!"*

Grandma: *"It's really getting you down."* (Grandma is reflective and just uses different words for "you are bored")

Amy: *"You bet."*

Grandma: *What's getting you the most?"* (A good it-question starts with *"What,"* instead of, *"Why are YOU so bored?"*)

Amy: *"I don't know. I guess it's the whole thing."*

Grandma: *"You need a break."* This is reflective of "the whole thing (is boring)" and is a sympathetic remark that avoids, "There must be something wrong (with you)!"

Amy: *"Yeah, but summer vacation is six weeks away."*

Grandma: *"Got any plans?"* (Good, puts the conversation on a positive topic.)

Amy: *"No."*

Grandma: *"Hard to think that far ahead."* (A reflective statement that just repeats "No plans" with sympathetic words)

Amy: *"Pam is looking for summer camps online."*

Grandma: *"Sounds like a good idea."* Avoids the quick evaluation of, "Camp might be expensive...it might be too early to apply, etc." Immediate negative evaluations only discourage the search for answers at this early stage.

Amy: *"I might go online and look for some myself."*

A complaint about boredom is a familiar remark to most grandparents. Although not much is solved about boredom in this conversation, Grandma has a better understanding of her granddaughter's feelings and has avoided the temptation to "get something done" in this short talk. Indirectly, Grandma said she has had similar feelings to her granddaughter's, and it's all right to have those. Most important, it's all right to tell Grandma about feelings without being criticized for feeling bored.

By allowing her granddaughter to direct the topic, information flowed to Grandma instead of from her, and she has a "ticket of admission" for next time:

"Say, did Pam ever get any camp applications?" or,

"Only five weeks left now; how's it going?"

Notice there is no room for adding old complaints in this approach. Avoid frequent criticisms such as, *"You shouldn't be bored," "You don't plan ahead like Pam,"* or out-of-left-field complaints such as, *"You spend too much time on the computer!" "You never do your homework!"* and *"You have bad friends!"* Such criticisms are too broad and will be taken personally because they say, *"And while I'm thinking about you, another thing I don't like is..."*

Instead, encourage your grandkids to take the conversational lead and postpone your own topics about mistakes. Later sections in this book will deal with those other bigger mistakes.

Help your grandchildren explore alternatives.

Reflecting their statements can help them get to a point of exploring alternatives to a problem and taking action to solve it. When a grandparent sends the message, *"I heard you,"* and *"It's all right to feel the way you do,"* your grandchild is likely to go beyond letting out feelings to considering, *"What can I do about it?"*

Grampa and grandma help most by tuning in to a grandchild's level of feeling and energy. Is he looking for alternatives, considering a particular one, or just letting out emotion? Grandparents must listen with empathy and react appropriately to give support. If a child is getting rid of emotion, a helpful grandparent reflects that. At other times a grandchild may be exploring the alternatives.

Megan: *"Those kids are always dissing me online. I don't know what to do."*

Grampa: *"What alternatives are there?"*

Kids are creative at listing options when they are ready. But if no idea comes up, the problem may not be clear yet, and your grandchild needs to explore more by expressing opinions and feelings.

Perhaps Megan is ready to try an alternative.

Megan: *"I'm going to tell those kids to quit bugging me!"*

Grampa: "*How do you think they'll react to that?*"

Megan: "*They might stop, but if they don't I'll just ignore them from now on.*"

Grampa: "*Just ignore them?*"

Megan: "*Yeah, that works every time!*"

Well, the ignoring strategy may not work all the time, but Megan is now encouraged to take control and is working on her own problem—that's a step toward growing up.

Distinguishing a child's level of emotion and energy and reacting with support requires practice and empathy. When in doubt resist the temptation to suggest solutions.

7. Suggest Solutions with Care.

We are always tempted to suggest solutions to our kid's problems: *"Why don't you . . ."* *"You should try..."* *"Don't be so . . ."* These statements are well intended, but they often strike the listener as pushy and superior. Most of us don't react kindly to solutions that are suggested too early.

If you told me you're frequently late for work because of traffic, and I said you should get up earlier or take another route, you might be offended. I was just trying to be efficient by giving quick advice. I just want to fix things—preferably quickly, but efficiency in conversation is for business meetings and TV shows—not family discussions.

Family conversation should be enjoyed; it's not a job to get out of the way so we can get on to the really important stuff. Children need time to talk to you. As one lonely son put it to me, *"If all they want is a project, why don't they take up a hobby?"*

As an example of the temptation to fix things too quickly, look at the following conversation:

Sarah: *"Life is so depressing. People are so bad."*

Grandma: *"I know it gets like that at times."*

Here's a good start. It may seem like a terrible start because the topic is so discouraging, but that's Sarah's choice. A terrible start would be for Grandma to fall to temptation and disagree with her granddaughter right away by trying to "set her straight" with the solution: *"You shouldn't talk like that; there are a lot of good people in the world!"*

This correction is tempting but unnecessary—Sarah knows her remark is extreme. Also, it's somewhat dishonest on Grandma's part because she knows Sarah is partly right. Since the statement has some potential for agreement, Grandma's reflective statement takes the side that puts her closer to Sarah. Let's see how it goes:

Sarah: *"It gets like that all the time at school."*

Grandma: *"There must be some times that are good at school."*

Not good, Grandma's saying, *"You're wrong,"* and it's too early in the conversation for the implied disagreement, authority, and solution expressed in this nudge. Let's take that back and try again:

Grandma: *"School's been bad lately, huh?"*

This is better because it's reflective without evaluating who's to blame; it keeps the conversation on a third entity where Sarah started it (not her fault; not Grandma's). The next remark from Sarah is likely to be informative about what the problem is at school. Grandma, if careful, will learn a lot, and Sarah will *"get it all out."*

In most conversations between adults, the suggestions are left out completely. We don't finish a conversation with a neighbor by saying, *"So we're agreed you'll cut the hedge at least every two weeks!"* or, *"So don't go roaring off in your car like that, it disturbs everyone!"*

Be satisfied that most conversations with your

grandkids, like those with your neighbors, will have no immediate conclusions or results. Leave out the closing comment in most of your conversations. If you try to be the "winner" in every talk, then you will always have to make someone a "loser."

8. Beware of Arguments for Entertainment.

Is the conversation just an argument with Grandma for entertainment? The answer to this is particularly important when the argument is really about what your offspring says, not what she does. Intentions are not actions, but they can produce entertaining arguments. Some of your grandchild's behavior in school and other places are away from your influence. It could be one reason school and other outside activities are her favorite topics.

A child's more obnoxious stories may be re-designed for your ears alone, just to push your button or get you to argue! Most of the time, your reaction should be plain vanilla, especially regarding abstract or distant situations.

Some of the best habits for grandparents are ones that help them stay alert to see and react to the best behavior of the kids.

Reflecting a child's statements can help move

him toward exploring alternatives and taking action to solve a problem. It helps when a grandparent sends messages, "I heard you" and "It's all right to feel the way you do." Then your granddaughter or son is likely to risk talking about possible answers to questions like: "What can I do about it?" or "What would help?" A grandparent helps most by tuning into the child's level of feeling and energy for the problem.

Grampa may listen with empathy and react appropriately to give support. If his grandson is just venting emotion, a helpful listener reflects that and does not give or push the child or teen to look for answers.

Lori: *"Mr. Factors is a terrible math teacher! He won't even let you ask a question."*

Grampa: *"Questions are important in math—to get the problems straightened out before going on."* Good. Grampa stays clear of who is right, Lori or Mr. Factors.

Lori: *"Sure. How can I learn if he won't answer the questions?"*

Grampa: *"Does he ever review?"*

Lori: *"Oh, sure, he reviews, but it's so fast nobody knows what he's talking about."*

Grampa: *"Why don't you go in after class?"* (Whoops, Grampa just took a superior view here. Lori may counter with, *"That won't work"* or *"I tried that."*)

Let's give Grampa a second chance:

Grampa: *"Why does he go so fast?"*

Lori: *"Who knows? What a jerk."* (Lori's voice is lower now, running out of steam for this topic.)

Grampa: *"Hmmm."* (always a good response in tricky situations)

Lori: *"Some teachers are so hard to deal with."*

Grampa: *"Hmmm, Yes."*

You may feel impatient with Grampa in this conversation. Why doesn't he help? Couldn't he at least encourage Lori to go in after class? Or encourage her to speak up insistently in class?

If this is the third complaint about Mr. Factors, Grampa might give some advice, but on the first round he should pass up the temptation to give advice and just let his granddaughter know he's on her side. How can she feel comfortable and spontaneous in bringing up sensitive topics and venting some steam if Grampa always takes the shortcut to a solution and "quick fix?"

38 - Dr. Roger McIntire

Suggestion 2: Avoid the Shortcuts
<u>Give</u> a nice day.

With so much competition from TV, CD's, social media, pod casts, talk shows and movies, chances for a talk with your grandchildren may become precious. When the opportunity comes up, here are some reminders.

The first priority in grandparenting should be finding things to highlight about our grandkids. If Grandma or Grampa zero in on the shortcut of looking for the obvious mistakes, blunders and bad behavior, they may miss the gems and successes. Reprimands are easy to think of. Compliments take more time.

As we react to what our grandchildren do, messages accumulate every day about what we like, and what we don't like. If you are on the lookout for bad behaviors, you may fail to notice opportunities to catch them being good--to show them you like them.

This can be one reason some growing granddaughters and sons become alienated from the family and would rather go outside with friends or stay in their own rooms. Often it is the likelihood of criticism, "put downs," and corrections that drives them away.

A habit of saying "I love you" is not much without frequent messages that say "I like you." Finding behaviors to like is the main business of parents and grandparents. Your habits are contagious, and your disposition is a part of the family atmosphere. If looking for mistakes becomes the routine, grandparents might not like the grandparenting job and look for ways to shorten the time spent. The family atmosphere follows that mood. Children will respond in kind, recycling the wrong attitude through the family.

Your grandchildren may engage in a conspiracy—almost unconsciously—to convince you that you are having no effect. But don't be misled. Your influence may not show up in the short run, but your reactions do make a difference. Don't give up. Attention, praise, and general encouragement are handy rewards. They should be used often.

Vague expectations about what good behavior is and specific descriptions of bad, lead to unbalanced messages that say "I don't like you" more often than they say, "I like you." Bad behavior may attract most of the attention because the "good" behavior is not spelled out well enough to be easily noticed. Getting down to the specifics of good behavior leads to many advantages.

For example, grandparents who are alert and praise the small successes that are the parts of larger accomplishments send clear messages about behavior. The kids develop and improve with small, easy steps instead of becoming discouraged by reprimands for little mistakes.

Developing a good child-grandparent relationship should be a part of every day interactions. Children long for the joy and safety of it; and grandparents take some satisfaction and pride in it. Your relationship is developing from a mixture of your understanding of what's going on, your messages, rules, listening, and your example. Consistent strategies are key ingredients in cultivating this relationship.

Basic heredity and personality will still show through in a growing family, but a review of daily events can often be useful because you can plan to withhold reactions and deliberately provide a positive model. The best outcome would be we all get what we deserve and improve our behavior as a result. Of course, out in the real world of our children, some justice is done, but undeserved rewards do occur, and satisfaction only happens to a degree.

1. One-ups and Put-downs are, too often, a Part of Shortcut Grandparenting.

Put-downs and one-ups disrupt useful family conversation. They give too much attention to winners and losers. Then both grandparents and parents have a tough time getting any information about the temptations and troubles the kids are facing.

Where does shortcut grandparenting lead? We all can have verbal habits and attitudes that can turn an otherwise valuable conversation into an argument.

Put-downs are a tempting shortcut to get Grandma's corrections across, but they are often too vague and personal. For example, vague complaints are sometimes triggered by a particular infraction, "Only ignorant people use that language." Of course he knows you're talking about a particular (usually four-letter) word, but, for impact, this objection has been expressed as an insult of the whole person.

Better to avoid the general put-down and focus on the present mistake. "Don't say that word in our family; it's rude, abusive, and as an adjective to 'car' it doesn't even make sense."

I agree this is still a put-down, but it is focused on the specific behavior not the whole person, and with some extra explanation, it is more constructive. This will not immediately take care of the problem, but at least your grandson may search for other words next time. When he finds them, let him know you are impressed. *"That's a good way to say that."*

One-upmanship is also a bad habit. It usually comes near the end of a conversation when we decide to declare ourselves the winner. We often like to see starts and ends where only a continuing process of change exists.

For example, we hope to persuade our grandchildren to avoid bad habits by not starting them. No smoking, no drugs, no alcohol.

Conclusions on the end of these conversations are better left off. *"So I don't ever want to hear that you..."* is better replaced by a reason, *"Once those brain cells are gone, they don't re-grow."*

These discussions will continue beyond the age of 20. The best help will be your reasoning against the bad habits and your example. Statistically, smoking kids come from smoking families.

Alcohol abuse breeds alcohol abuse—regardless of Grandma's and Grampa's rationalizations or excuses for their own behavior. Children copy better than they listen.

Here's another example.

Grandma: *"You can't quit school. You won't get anywhere without an education."*

Grandson: *"They don't teach anything I need to know."*

Now Grandma could remain inflexible, stay with put-downs and disagree, saying her grandson needs to learn the basics and doesn't know what needs to be learned.

She could also go with a one-up. *"Your mother wouldn't have the job she has today if she had quit, and I would never have been a teacher without extra schooling."*

A better approach might be to look for agreement. Certainly there's more to learn since we were in school. Maybe he is right about what he needs to know, and it's time to look to the school for a better menu. Just working out what else needs to be learned may help him start learning it, whether the school decides to teach it or not.

We can easily slip into office-candidate modes with our own grandchildren, but unlike political campaigns where only the candidates are judged, at home everyone is in for the long haul. Everyone is a player on stage. This makes a big difference.

Conversation should not be a game. In games, for every winner, we imply there is also a loser. If grandparents play to win, the games will be short because older people have more practice putting everything into words. Sooner or later Grandma and Grampa will not be able to find a "loser" who wants to play.

"How was school?"

"Same old thing."

Grandma has a choice right away. She could say, *"Come on, something must have happened."* Grandma's score is up one, granddaughter's is down one. Or Grandma could leave the score at zero saying, *"Gets pretty dull in the middle of the year."*

"Yeah, everybody's going nuts having to stay inside all day—even for soccer practice."

Now Grandma could say something else agreeable and understanding, *"This weather has certainly been awful."* Or she could play to win,

"Well, at least you have more time to get your homework done." Grandma's score is up one again, but her granddaughter's alarm goes off. Here comes Grandma's favorite topic and criticism. Granddaughter's defenses are activated. It's easy to slip into this shortcut mode.

Better to forget about the ending and let most conversations explore situations without conclusions. Neither side wants instructions anyway.

Another disadvantage to adversarial games with children is that losers quickly become non-risk takers. Then creativity goes down, and conversations increasingly become defensive and short. Sometimes both sides end up just attacking and defending

Sometimes, we grandparents suspect that these confrontations have become a habit and an entertainment for our grandchild. They are inefficient encounters for a child looking for the satisfaction of dominating at least in a conversation at home.

You don't have to be drawn into these tennis-game conversations. It isn't necessary to return every argument with a retort. Take your time with reactions as you would with an adult. Just, *"Hmmm"* or *"Ahhh"* is often enough. Avoid the personal comments as much as possible and encourage your offspring to think (and talk) like an adult.

With the time-limit ignored and the score left at zero, future talks will be more frequent, more productive and probably more interesting.

Family shortcuts can make us feel we are protecting and disciplining the kids when we are actually giving no specific help or instructions at all.

"You need to try a little harder to be nice at these family gatherings."

"Your manners were terrible, and you should be nicer to your cousins."

"You had better shape up and make an effort, Jeff."

Grampa's well-intended advice to Jeff is of little help. Trying harder, showing better manners, being nicer, shaping up and even making an effort are not specific. They could strike a child-teenager as magical ideas.

These general directions leave enough loopholes to allow Jeff to avoid any new effort and still have room to defend himself later. Better to be specific and say, *"When your aunt asks you about school, stop and answer her."* Better yet, *"Stop and tell her about your science project."* The specific suggestion is no longer magical, and if Jeff takes the advice, he can be more pleasant next time.

Sometimes we engage in magic to avoid direct confrontation and sometimes because we have no answers. We only know we want things to be better. One Grampa said to me, *"He knows what I mean. I don't have to spell it out for him."* Vague criticism makes it easy for Grampa, but it is confusing for a child.

"Jeff, you had better start acting right."
"What did I do?"
"You're always fighting with your sister."
"She starts it."
"Well, you'd better learn to get along."

Not much information in this exchange. What is "acting right?" What strategy should Jeff learn to "get along" besides the one he has already selected—blame the problems on his sister?

Better to quit this game of grandparent-child dodge ball and be specific, *"Jeff, when your sister calls you names, tell her you won't talk to her when she does that and then leave."* Will this advice solve the problem? Probably not, but a specific plan gives Jeff a little more control and Grampa a way to be truly helpful.

Separating sister and brother is sometimes necessary but doesn't teach much. It just satisfies Grampa (or Grandma) with a temporary stop to the arguing. Grampa's guilt is relieved because he has "done something" about the problem.

Often it's our definitions, or lack of them, that get us into trouble. *"OK, you can ride your motorbike out on the road, but be careful."* What does "be careful" mean? Go slow? The whole idea of getting on the road is to go faster. These two are going to have another argument about the motorbike. Grampa should be specific or refuse to let him use the road.

To make real progress, Grampa will need to identify the actions of his grandson that will directly contribute to a better adjustment. Usually this requires coming up with specific and clear alternatives to bad behavior.

The best advice you can give a grandchild is your example, without advice. It's the best control you have in arguments. If you lower your voice, your grandchildren will lower theirs, and you'll have a better chance to get your suggestions across to them.

Girls and boys need any encouragement we can give, and the most useful encouragement will be your time—time for sharing stories, talking over weekend plans and time to look over a grandchild's latest project. Don't be discouraged by a teenager's apparent indifference toward these activities. Kids often feel obligated to act independent (I don't need any homework help) and competent (I know all about how to use that computer) with both their parents and their grandparents.

In these conversations, remember that often a child's number one fear is embarrassment. Avoid beginning with a question you know they can't answer, *"How are you going to learn if you don't pay attention?"* Start with information they might want, *"Here's a program on TV about those African lions. What part of Africa do they live in? Maybe we could find it on a map."*

Don't be too busy for mealtime talk. Mealtimes can provide a snapshot of general family happiness, but many families have given up the tradition. Breakfast is either nonexistent or taken on the run in the morning rush. Lunch takes place at either school or work. Shawn eats dinner by herself in front of the TV. Her big sister snacks and sends text messages to friends. Grampa and Grandma eat supper while watching the news. Little time could be left for serious talk.

Without mealtime practice, both grandparents and kids forget how to talk to each other. Family conversation is reduced to sound bytes. Big mistakes can result.

Often, grandparents may see their grandchildren only at holiday and special occasions. This is where grandparents can make sure the festive meal allows every one a part in preparation and the conversation.

Are you too busy for a slow pace? Most of our social habits are learned from our parents' (or grandparents') example and will not be learned by the kids if we are too busy to sit down and take time with supper. *"They've got to learn to shift for themselves,"* one Grandma told me. What choices will they make, and who will teach them to "shift for themselves?"

When you have a chance to share a meal with the grandkids, deliberately use a slow pace, no newspaper, no TV, no mobile devices. This is a great time for family stories. Avoid starting remarks with "you," don't try to steer the conversation, don't try to "win" and, oh yes, don't expect changes in the first month.

The crucial question confronting grandparents is not whether they will use rewards, punishments, encouragements, and discouragements to influence their grandchildren. In day-to-day living that influence is inevitable. The question is whether grandparents will have time for thoughtful reactions that will contribute to their grandchildren's development and provide an enjoyable companionship while growing up.

The emphasis on the defects in the person will act as a punishment. Jovial and approachable people never seem to punish. They seem to have a rule that says, *"When mistakes happen, emphasize <u>outside events.</u>"* The habit is contagious, and the whole family atmosphere is more positive.

If looking for mistakes becomes the routine, grandparents may become unpleasant, and they may not like themselves after a visit.

Grandparents and their grandsons and daughters should be friends. Not in the sense of enjoying the same music or having friends in common, but through enjoying time together and supporting the strengths and successes of each other.

Friends bring out the best in me. When we meet, their attention sweeps the common ground between us looking for sparkles to highlight. I like the "me" they draw out. I return the compliment, like a friendly searchlight, seeking the best in them.

Some people have another focus. Their search overlooks the good in me and zeros in on vulnerable spots. I pull back and risk very little. I know what they're looking for. I cover up.

Aim *your* searchlight carefully. What are you looking for?

2. Who Deserves the Blame Or the Credit?

We usually give credit for successes, but for mistakes and failure, we distribute the blame in one of two ways: For *our own* mistakes we usually choose "outside blame" that finds the explanation in circumstances. This makes us unfortunate victims of situations outside of ourselves, *"It was so noisy in there, how could anyone think or be able to do the right thing?"* "Outside blame" also includes people, *"I was too distracted because people were coming so late!"*

When it comes to the mistakes of *other people,*

we are tempted to use "inside blame." *"What* (inside condition) *makes him so inconsiderate, so clumsy? Why doesn't she pay more attention? What was she thinking of?"*

Inside blame is a dangerous habit. It leads to frustration because a child is viewed as "having" (inside) an almost unchangeable character.

Outside blame leads parents and grandparents to look for problem *situations* instead of problem *kids*. With a good understanding of a problem situation, you have a chance to support a workable solution, and that, in turn, gives your grandkids a new chance. In order to plan reactions to problem situations, we need a clear view of what's happening. Blaming your grandchildren doesn't help because it makes assumptions about what is going on inside.

Nick:: *Grandma, you said you'd take me to the pool. can we go now?*

Grandma: *"Just a minute, Nicholas, I'm listening to your mother."*

Nick: *"But I've been waiting all morning."*

Grandma: *"Just a minute!"*

Nick: *We need to leave right now!"*

Grandma: *"A minute ago you were watching TV, now we have to drop everything and rush."*

Nick: *"Forget it. I just won't go."*
Grandma: *"Just get in the car, OK?"*
Nick: *"OK, if you insist."*
Grandma: *"What!?"*
Later, Grandma says: *"Nick is so selfish. He sits around watching TV, then demands immediate service, no matter what! It drives me crazy!"*

Grampa: *"Maybe he is selfish, but we could try a rule that says all rides from us require a 5-minute warning before take-off time. And any time he tries abusing us like that we should just say, Well, if you really don't mind not going, OK!"*

Grandma: *"You're right. Going to the pool is less important than giving him the message he can't twist us around like that."*

Grandpa: *"It might not always come out perfect, but at least we will take back a little control of the situation."*

Instead of fixing the blame inside Nick (he's selfish), Grampa suggested they try changing their reactions to Nick when he makes a demand. It could be Nick is doing it for attention, and even an argument about his demanding nature could be rewarding.

The complaint that Nicholas is *"too demanding*

and selfish" refers to real actions of Nicholas but also implies the problem is part of his nature. The result is that the blame has been put inside Nicholas, and his grandparents may believe that any change can only come from there.

The *"Why?"* of a child's behavior is best answered by changing *"Why?"* to *"What happens next?"* Nicholas makes an inconsiderate demand and then what happens? His ride comes through *and* any disruption is blamed on Grandma for not cooperating on demand. What different consequence could be planned? The answer is not always simple and obvious, but Grandma starts at the right place by looking for a solution instead of blaming Nicholas. This approach is more productive than giving up and just labeling him "selfish."

The new focus may lead to a plan to support Nick's considerate behavior and to exercise caution in reacting to his little traps.

Grandma can be on the lookout to give credit for the good accomplishments of her grandson (or daughter), but she may feel these opportunities are few and far between. The problem may be partly due to the way behaviors are described. If good behaviors are only vaguely defined, they are less likely to occur and be recognized. Deciding just when to support a child may not be easy:

Matt (age 13): *"I got my room cleaned up."*
Grandma: *"Great!"*
Matt: *"I didn't pick up the parts to my model because I'm not finished with it yet"*

Here's a crucial moment for Grandma. Her choices are: continue support for what was done; after all, half a loaf is better than none, or hold out for a higher standard and only give credit when the whole job, with the model put away, is done, and the credit is due.

A definition of what is acceptable would help; doesn't Matt have the option of leaving one ongoing project out? Grandma will have to make this judgment of Matt's progress and potential, but his habit should be to err to the side of encouragement—there are few circumstances in adult-rearing where there is a danger of an overdose of support.

Another concern for Grandma is what kind of credit should she give? "Outside credit" may be "no credit" (encouragement) at all for Matt: *"I guess the mess finally got to you. Even _you_ couldn't stand it anymore."*

So Grandma gives the credit to Matt's environment for driving Matt to do the right thing, not much self-esteem in that approach. But also, Grandma shouldn't take the credit herself by saying, *"Well now, didn't I tell you that would be better?"* Grandma should send the credit directly to Matt for getting the job done:

Grandma: *"Well, you still need the model out; you would have to just about wreck it to put it away. You (not me, and not other influences) have it looking really good in here!"*

3. Look for Needs Instead of Blames.

Recognizing the priorities of needs can sometimes explain the otherwise puzzling fate of some rules. For example, I worked with two very different sisters whose reactions to cleaning up their rooms were very confusing.

Michelle needed to be constantly assured that she was capable and successful, and she tried hard to be cooperative and helpful. Her sister Susan also seemed to value approval but wanted prolonged attention and companionship more than praise.

A rule that reminded Grandma to praise both daughters for keeping their rooms nice worked well for Michelle seeking confirmation of a job well done. Since attention ended when the rooms were done, attention-seeking Susan procrastinated in doing her part just to keep the cleaning going on and on. Susan prolonged the room-cleaning chores for the attention she received—even negative attention would do—while our more goal-directed Michelle worked hard for the confirmation of her success.

Grandma may want her granddaughters to clean up their rooms to keep the place looking nice, but why does she have to be right on top of them while they do it? The reason may be that while she thinks having a nice room is the point of the clean-up (a long-term goal), her granddaughters' priorities may be quite short-term—one wants assurance that she is contributing (doing it right); the other wants attention for doing any work at all!

Grandma has *two* strategies to work on. One strategy Grandma carries out deliberately—encourage them when they clean their rooms;

the other strategy is an unintentional one of giving unusual attention to Susan's procrastination. So Susan *slows up* for attention, but Michelle *finishes up* for praise.

The solution for Michelle and Susan came with the insight that Susan needed attention at the end and long after the chores were completed. This attention did not need to be in the form of praise for room-cleaning; it just needed to continue in order to show Susan that finishing the room didn't finish Grandma's attention.

It would be a mistake to conclude that Michelle wants to please Grandma and Susan doesn't. Or that Susan just wants to aggravate her grandmother. These conjectures about sinister Susan would only lead to more nagging and a sour turn in Grandma's relationship with Susan. Grandma is the adult and *she* has to make the special effort, after room-cleaning, to show interest in Susan.

4. Avoid the Temptation to Increase the Blame as They Grow Up.

As children become teenagers, blaming them is increasingly tempting for grandparents, *"They're old enough to know better!"* This habit can distract grandparents from looking for a chance to give personal credit when it is deserved. For example, you might know a teenager who is moody, disrespectful, rebellious, or cynical. This might be a "long-standing habit" (inside blame) and we might think, *"That's just the way he has always been."* But even older teens act the way they do partly because of the way they expect to be treated—because of what has ordinarily happened next.

Teens may be disrespectful because the only time they are taken seriously is when they act disrespectful, or their bad behavior may produce an entertaining argument, or their bad talk may seem more "adult" than saying something pleasant. Even some adults believe that!

When a disrespectful teen turns happy and cheerful, adults may pat him on the head and tell him he's a "nice boy" but otherwise ignore him. The usefulness of bad behavior in this situation is not lost on a grumpy teen.

Showing respect for a grandchild by asking for his opinion and showing confidence in his abilities will bring out an improved form of respect in return. This strategy will be an example to be modeled, and it encourages an attitude that will replace "disrespectful."

Grandma: *"It's too early for a garden outside, but we could start seeds inside. What do you think, Nick?"*

Nick: *"What good would that do?"*

Grandma: *"Later, when we plant them outside, they would have a head start."*

Nick: *"Even melons and stuff like that?"*

Grandma: *"Even melons. Let's do melons."*

5. "I Always Felt I Was Never Good Enough."

While talking with two fellow Grampas about our growing-up years, one Grampa said, *"I always felt I was never quite good enough,"* He said that after he had a family of his own he wrote a letter to his dad every week throughout his adult years. His father criticized each for leaving out some detail. "I wish he had just once said that he appreciated the family news. He never wrote me, but he always called and pointed out some person or subject that had been left out of my latest letter."

Many of us never experience such deserved appreciation, but the greater tragedy is that while a grandparent holds back compliments, the kids become discouraged and resentment sets in. It takes courage to overcome the disadvantage of a family that was too stingy with compliments. Grandparents can be the ones providing the encouragement when parents cannot or will not.

The short-term job is child-rearing, but the long-term goal is adult-rearing. To reach that goal, children need examples of how adults handle their responsibilities and accomplish their tasks. But the kids are not adults yet, and left to their own inclinations, they may miss their chances to learn. They need a lot of time just following along while the adults show them the ways of the world.

How a child grows into the independence and competency of adulthood varies from family to family and we all know that the extent of success varies also. We could probably agree that, ideally, child-rearing should be a process of gradually expanding responsibility and independence. Unfortunately, we have all seen many families where the children go through a long period of severe limits followed by an abrupt and risky freedom at about the age of 17 when the American teenager is sprung from the nest to go to college or work.

Grandma: *"I need some help with thanksgiving dinner. Neal, could you set the table for everyone?"*

Neal (age 5): *"Do I hafta? Make Dawn do it."*

Grandma: *"No, Dawn is making the potato casserole. You can set the table."*

Neal: *"I'd rather make a casserole like Dawn."*

Grandma: *"OK. next time you visit, we'll go over how to do that. But for now, set the table. That will be a great help!"*

I am sure Neal isn't completely happy with this chore, but with the proper appreciation, he will have an additional feeling of worth and ability.

While parents usually talk to their offspring about the demands of the outside world, and grandparents support them, it is easy to forget to allow practice with as much of that reality as possible. As soon as reasonable, children need experience with taking care of themselves. Helping with meals is a good place to start.

When they are successful, the protection of the extended family nest can make sure that the success is recognized and encouraged. The failures can be learning experiences with the consequences softened by family. A long period of safe trial and error is possible for children whose families allow for it.

Suggestion 3: Watch Out for the Games
Every time we win, we make a loser

When a child puts his electronic entertainment aside, he may look for entertainment somewhere else. Maybe a game with Grandma or a conflict with a sibling will provide a fun game.

"Don't play games with me!" an aggravated grandparent will say. But everyone plays a few games, and the best way to deal with a game is to recognize what your grandchildren's purpose is in the game, and how you want to play it.

1. What Games?
Game 1: "Referees Are Fun"

Steven: *"Grandma! Mark won't turn down his music!"*

Grandma: *"Mark, turn it down. Steven needs to get his homework done."*

Mark: *"He's not doing his homework, he's just goofing around with it."*

Steven: *"Grandma! Mark still has it too loud!"*

Grandma: *"Steven, it sounds OK to me now."*

Mark: *"Grandma, Steve came in and turned off my music!"*

Steven: *"Grandma, Mark pushed me!"*

Mark: *"To get you out of my room, I have to push."*

Grandma: *"You two cut that out! Mark, get out here right now! If I have to come in there..."*

In this game, Grandma is referee. You can almost hear someone yell, *"Hey, Ref! Call those penalties and control the game!"* It's safer than regular conflict because you can count on Grandma, the Ref, to call a halt to the escalation. By the way, as all basketball and soccer grandparents know, referees (I was a soccer referee for 20 years) are usually wrong 50 percent of the time from each player's (or grandparent's) point of view. So if you lose, you can always blame the referee—what a nice way to pass time or procrastinate on doing homework!

Why don't adults play this game? Sometimes they do, of course. It's just that the third party (the referee) can't be counted on to keep the game going or to intervene when the conflict gets hot. Once the referee leaves the game or fails to play the role of protector, the players have to quit or play by their rules.

Most referees are tempted to coach now and then, and grandparents are no different.

"Mark, why don't you let Steven do his homework and play your music later?" Suggestions are usually resented partly because the game would be over.

The resolution can't be perfect for the kids. But Grandma's goal here is to get herself out of the referee role and give responsibility back to the boys. The less-than-perfect solution can be fixed any time the brothers want to fix it. Many of these games become much less troublesome to grandparents when they identify how the game is being played and change their reactions to give control back to the players.

If the suggested solution is rejected, Grandma could always end the game by removing the source of the conflict—Mark's music or Steven's selected place for doing homework. If Grandma remains stern, she might insist the boys use one of her solutions. The danger here is that if Grandma is not stern, her solutions will only become a new source for more "fun and games,"

Game 2: "I'll Bet You Can't Make Me Happy"

Here is a game that also pulls grandparents into the problems of their grandchildren when the kids should be taking responsibility.

"Grandma, what can I do? I'm bored."

"Why don't you finish your art project?"

"I've done most of it, and it's not coming out right."

"Well, how about helping me with the garden?"

"That's just work."

"Well, then, you might as well get your homework done."

"I don't have to do it yet"

"Well, why don't you..."

Many grandparents recognize this conversation as one that has no end. There will be continuing attention from Grandma as long as no suggestion is right.

Suppose old hard-headed Uncle Harry and his friend, Al, came over and started this game with Grandma? She would probably make a few suggestions, and then since they are adults, she would think it was time for the adults to entertain themselves!

Grandma can't win the *"I'll-bet-you-can't-make-*

me-happy" game, but after a few suggestions, she can pass the responsibility back to "the kids."

Game 3: "My Problem is Your Problem"

This is a common game of a child that will develop in the later teenage years into *"Help me because you're in charge."* As with many of these games, frankly stating the fair truth may stop the game and allow some real progress.

"I can't find my cell phone, Grandma!"

"Maybe it's on the hall table, Tyler."

"I already looked there."

"Why don't you try upstairs?"

"Grandma, it's supposed to be down here, could you go look?"

"Hold it, Tyler, you go upstairs easier than I. Don't make this my problem."

This game has a little of the flavor of the *"I'll-bet-you-can't-make-me-happy"* game. In both cases attention from Grandma looks suspiciously like the reward that's prolonging the game, and it's time to put Tyler on his own for awhile to search for solutions.

Game 4: "If You Really Loved Me, You Would Serve Me."

Here's a game that is similar to the *"My-Problem-is-Your-Problem"* game with a little extra pull on the guilt strings of Grampa or Grandma.

Michael: *"Grandma, I need those shoes!"*

Grandma: *"Michael, I told you. You have a pair of running shoes—one pair is enough."*

Michael: *"But these are different. Matthew's Grandma got him a pair."*

Grandma: *"I said one pair is enough—it's too much money."*

Michael: *"Matthew's Grandma said they're worth it for <u>her</u> grandson!"*

Grandma: *Michael, don't run that guilt trip on me. I'm the one who bought you the first pair, remember?"*

Calling Michael on his attempt to blame his Grandma for his troubles will not stop this argument, but when Grandma recognizes the game, she can keep the proper view of the talk and not let her *grandson* get control of *her* emotions.

Game 5: "I May Do Something Bad!"

"I may do something bad" is a game where a

child *talks* about wild intentions just for the attention of the moment. When you suspect this game, you can try to inhibit your strong reactions to his verbal description of his intentions and concern yourself only with the problem at the moment. Without a strategy, your offspring may find it easy to "get through" to you by making a remark about some absurd behavior he has no intention of performing.

In the *"I may do something bad"* game, getting a child to "talk right" sometimes becomes the goal of Grandma or Grampa, and that part becomes the power struggle. Little talks may become unproductive, because if your grandchild starts to lose he can always say (promise) what is being demanded without having to carry it through. Threats may be made, voices raised, and your grandchild may get a good "talking to," but he will only learn to say what is necessary to avoid any genuine discussion of controversial topics.

Game: 6: "This is Not Perfect!"

Sandra: *"These art museums are boring."* (That is, this activity is not good or perfect.)

Grandma: *"Some of these paintings are very famous and beautiful."*

Sandra: *"They're all old pictures of old people."*

Grandma: *"But look at this one. Can you see how the artist used light and dark to show how the light comes from the candle?"*

Sandra: *"I could do that."*

Grandma: *"And look at this one. Look how some things are made to look far away and some closer."*

Sandra: *"They're just smaller."*

Grandma: *"But they are just the right sizes, and a little less clear."*

Sandra: *"I guess."*

Is Sandra getting a new appreciation of art? Be careful in concluding that Sandra's museum trip is a waste of time just because she thinks your place to go was not the "perfect" one. Remember, sometimes kids feel an obligation to make you believe you are having no effect. Later on, when Sandra encounters other art or tries out her own painting skills again, you may get a better indication of the usefulness of the museum trip. Keep your own spirits up on the museum trip even if things are not going perfectly. Guard against copying your grandchild's gloomy attitude. More may be getting done than you realize.

Regardless of your approach to child-rearing, or adult-rearing as I like to call it, the question of whether anything has changed in the mind of the child or teenager will remain partially unanswered. All your efforts will probably seem only partly successful. Children, seeking proof that they are persons in their own right, want it that way!

2. Listening During the Game.

Good listening skills are crucial to handling games that the kids play. All the rules of Suggestion 1 apply here. When the conversation starts, look at your grandson or daughter rather than a TV screen or newspaper. To deal with any of these games you need to focus your attention on it. Turn and face him or her so there is no impression that you will miss what's really going on. These physical aspects of your attention let your grandchild know you're paying attention and not likely to be fooled by a game.

Feedback of what your children just said is a good habit during these conversations. Let your grandchild know that you heard what he or she said by repeating it. Avoid suggesting solutions in these games. They may only lead to *"make-me-happy"* or *"my-problem-is-yours."* Also, suggesting solutions makes you sound superior and tempts your game-player to counter with something different just to stay even.

3. Watch for a Chance to Encourage Something Better.

Anyone who has ever tried to play a musical instrument, improve in a sport, or raise children knows that just talking about it is not enough. Reading, lecturing and memorizing rules can help, but real practice is crucial! Even golf has helpful hints and rules to learn, but all golfers know the only way to improve is through practice. And all golfers know players who still search for the magic gadget or secret technique for success while they avoid practice time. The notion applies equally well to social behavior, controlling anger, getting along with siblings, homework, tooth-brushing, and money management!

So helping a child listen and pay attention to advice is not enough, he will have to try out your instruction, test your rules, and then, if the consequences and encouragements are there, he will learn. The progress itself—the result—will have to come from practice. This is an important role of the family—to provide a place where successful practice is supported, and mistakes receive only constructive reactions—not a likely experience in the outside world.

4. Careful Messages for Grandsons and Daughters.

We often show expectations of gender differences in our questions and opinions of the behavior of children. A bias in these expectations can reduce the self-confidence of a girl interested in an area traditionally "masculine." It can also delay development of social skills in a boy if he is excused from social obligations because he's "a naturally immature boy." The bias can slip in early. Be on the lookout for it. Note the gender biases in the following table.

Child #1	Child #2
Are you happy?	Are you successful?
Are you acting right?	Did you win?
Is your homework perfect?	Is your homework done?
Is your hair attractive?	Is your hair combed?
Are your shoes shined?	Where are your shoes?
Don't eat too much.	Don't eat too little.
Sleep, you look tired.	Sleep, you act tired.
Exercise to look better.	Exercise to be stronger.
Have friends.	Do sports.

Be friendly.   Be competent.
Be attractive.   Be productive.

In spite of the recent emphasis on gender equality, our expectations of boys and girls differ; boys and girls develop different capacities and motivations, and the world has different expectations of them. Whether the characteristics are inborn or learned, I'm sure you needed no extra hint to recognize that Child #1 was a girl, and Child #2 was a boy.

We often emphasize different values and different aspects of growing up for boys and girls, partly out of consideration for them and partly out of our desire to prepare them for a world we know still has sexist expectations. Sometimes our emphasis is in the best interest of our son or daughter, sometimes not.

Grandparents usually react to a boy by directing him toward success with the tasks at hand and by placing less emphasis on social relationships. Usually we encourage girls to succeed socially and give only the necessary minimum emphasis to the task at hand. Pressuring boys about being winners and girls about being charmers may produce stress that will be resented. It also risks a reaction by your grandchildren of proving your values wrong, *"I don't have to win (or be perfect), and I'll prove it, I'll quit!"* A person who pushes too hard for a perfect student or a perfect charmer may end up with a school or social dropout.

The job for grandparents, parents and teachers is to carefully separate fact from prejudice. Children need to be encouraged to try many skills, develop interests and abilities into strengths, and enjoy successes. The sources of sex differences are in both the environment and our heredity. Records of school problems with boys reflect these differences.

A grandparent's role is to avoid unrealistic expectations and unfair limitations created by gender stereotypes while remaining alert for opportunities to help the kids learn by practice. Taking a risk and trying out new tasks may be influenced by your grandchild's self-confidence, partly acquired from family. Gender biases of parents and grandparents will partly determine how much practice a child will risk, and how much encouragement he will experience.

"OK," Mr. Effort said, *"Everybody make two lines at the side of the exercise mats. If you want*

to practice the standing exercises, get in the line near the windows. Those who want to practice handsprings, line up over here."

Donna's friend: *"Come on, Donna, I'll help you with the flip."*

"Flip?"

"The handspring. Com'on, I'll help you."

"You can get hurt doing that."

"You can get hurt getting off the bus!"

"Naw, it's mostly boys over there. Anyway, I'm not very good at that sort of thing."

"OK, but I'm going over. Mr. Effort said I'm getting pretty good for a girl."

So Donna's friend went to do handsprings, and Donna started for the floor exercises. Floor exercises were boring to Donna, but she felt safe with her own gender and safe from embarrassing mistakes.

Donna's expectation of herself determined what she practiced, and her expectation grew from many seeds planted by parents, grandparents and teachers. She was given a choice, and she decided to practice merely what she did best—a habit many of us have. She was intimidated from trying handsprings perhaps because of adult implications. Or perhaps she has learned from experience that she doesn't have the athletic ability for handsprings and could be hurt trying. Certainly kids have the right to apply their own common sense.

But if her timidity came from cautions and lowered expectations suggested by adults merely because she is a girl, then she has been tempted away from her potential, and another opportunity to gain self-esteem has slipped by.

Did Mr. Effort really tell Donna's friend she was pretty good *"for a girl?"* Or was the sexist qualification added by a girl who has become wise to the ways of the world? Whether spoken or presumed, she's a strong person to focus on the encouraging part of the remark and continue her practice.

Let's look at a male example:

Teacher: *"Today I want to check the sketches of plants you began outside yesterday."* The art teacher starts to visit from desk to desk.

Jim: *"Hey John, let me have one of your sketches to show Mrs. Aesthetic."*

John: *"Use your own, Jim."*

Jim: *"Com'on John, I only need one. I threw mine out when we came in yesterday—I'm no good at this artsy stuff."*

John: *"Do another. She won't be here for a while."*

Jim: *"I told you, I'm no good at this artsy stuff!"*

John: *"You don't even try, Jim."*

Jim: *"Oh yeah? I'll see you outside!"*

Has a boy like Jim, who says he's no good at "artsy stuff," been sold on his own weaknesses by a prejudiced society? Is he "no good" because he lacks potential, or has he been convinced he's "no good" by the same sexism that might have told Donna to stick with floor exercises?

5. Encourage Enjoyment of Success.

Grandma and Grampa stop to pick up their two grandchildren from school.

First child: *"I got my math papers back today, and I got more right than anyone!"*

Grampa: *"Wow, that's great. I hope you'll have time this weekend to study so you can keep ahead of the others."*

First child: *"Oh, I can keep ahead of them easy."* (Does the competitive attitude tell you this person is a boy?)

Grampa: *"Just knuckle down, and you'll get it."*

First child: *"I have another decimals

assignment tonight."

Grampa: *Well, if you want to stay at the top, you have to keep at it."*

Second child: *"Mrs. Brown said we have to choose a final project for home-ec: a cooking or sewing project."*

Grandma: *"Cooking can be fun."*

Second child: *"My friend Jennie is doing cooking, but I'm better with sewing."*

Grandma: *"Wouldn't you rather be with Jennie?"*

Second child: *"I guess you're right."*

Regardless of the sexes of these two students, one is encouraged to be concerned with success, while the other is encouraged to be comfortable.

Questionnaires about adult attitudes toward children tell us that the person in the math class is likely to be a boy, and the one who is encouraged to worry about friends before projects, a girl—at least their grandparents are treating them that way. There is no mistake here, merely an example of common family conversation where grandparents should be sensitive to their own reactions. Then they can encourage each child to develop his/her very best potential, without too much concern for fitting into common molds.

How will others treat your grandchildren? Most people will not treat them any better than their family does! Everyone in the family sets the tone for your friends and relatives on how the kids are treated in the outside world. Other adults will react to the collection of skills, presumptions, and attitudes your children have acquired. In your school years, *your expectations were partly acquired from your parents' and grandparents'* attitudes, and the foundation of your self-concept was begun. As an adult, you pass along that information—those assumptions about the good in yourself and the good in others—modified by the valuable experience you are willing to add to their own experience.

From that, your grandchild will develop an expectation about how others will perceive him. This becomes a self-fulfilling cycle of expectations because he or she has acquired a pattern of attitudes, assumptions, and habits that will be *re*created in new acquaintances and repeated from the experiences he left behind.

Most people won't treat your grandchildren any *worse* than you do, either! People model each other, and their reactions tend to create their surroundings.

Each of us cause some people to fade away and others to draw closer. We feather our own social nest.

Grandchildren will add your example of how you treat each person. Of course, parents will have the greatest impact, but your attitude, disposition, and the nature of your appetite for life will add to their personality also. Then they will be off to create their own social environment by reacting in ways both you and their parents would find familiar. Without giving it much attention, they will present an example built on their experience, modified by their parents' model—and your example as well.

84 - Dr. Roger McIntire

Solution 4: Careful With Punishment; It has Great Disadvantages

You Can't Make a Garden Just By Pulling Weeds.

Punishment is a tempting strategy when bad behavior demands immediate reaction, and the long-term relationship with your grandchild is temporarily less important. But punishment doesn't deliver the needed information about what a child needs *to do*. You can't make a garden just by pulling weeds; you have to plant something, grow something, nurture something.

The family needs to be a place where training through trial-and-error is encouraged and guided. This is the opposite of what is created when punishment is used.

"You're too easy on the kids! Let me have them for a week. They'll shape up after a couple of swats from their Grampa!" Nancy and Martin are a sister and brother team who started their game when they were four. They know all the buttons to push to get

the reactions they want. They're still playing their game of *"Let's-see-how-much-we-can-get-away-with."* They either conspire to work their parents up, or they bug each other and get parent attention as a bonus. Any suggestion to Nancy or Martin by their parents that they do *"something useful"* is rejected, perhaps because that would mean the game would be over.

1. Ten Reasons "Get Tough" Advice from Tough Grampa is Off Track.

Many of the relatives, including Grampa, think they could fix the Nancy-and-Martin problem with stern talk and extra punishments—restrictions or removed privileges. Grampa thinks he would somehow use punishment more effectively and more consistently than Nancy's and Martin's parents.

Reason #1: The Hard-Line Approach Will Be, Must Be, Inconsistent.

The first problem with Grampa's use of the straight punishment rule is that even Grampa cannot, *and should not*, be consistent with it. Punishment would be too inhuman without the inconsistencies of warnings and threats.

If Grampa's reactions could be as consistent and as quick as, say, an electric shock from a wall outlet or lamp socket, he might make some short-term progress.

Wall outlets and lamp sockets will consistently punish us without warning; they don't hesitate because we look cute trying to be "devilish." They don't think we've had a bad day or haven't been reminded lately of what will happen if we mishandle them. We get none of this consideration, and we are careful not to mistreat outlets and lamp sockets.

But Grampa is not a wall outlet. Out of love and sympathy neither Grandma, Grampa, nor any other member of the family can resist preceding punishments with the warnings and threats, and so the game begins. When the kids were younger, spankings might have been used. But you can't spank the big ones, and anyway, even spanking would have to include lots of warnings.

Consistency is always desirable and basic to learning. The lack of consistent reactions, on the reward side, leads to confusion and slows the progress. The inevitable inconsistency of punishment brings on additional problems.

Remember that "mean" teacher you had in school? Mr. Meany, or maybe it was a Ms. Meany, used punishments, reprimands, sarcastic remarks, put-downs and embarrassments whenever the kids deviated from the desirable, and sometimes even when it seemed the kids had done nothing wrong! I bet you hated that class!

A student's greatest fear is to be embarrassed. With "Mr. Meany," you just couldn't be sure when you might trigger an embarrassing reaction. *All* behaviors (even volunteering right answers, suggestions, or questions) were reduced, because you and your friends just wouldn't risk it. Not surprisingly, many "mean" teachers think the students in their classes are not very smart.

When punishment is uncertain, students become very cautious, especially when they are around the potential punisher. Around other people, bad behavior may increase to let off the oppressed steam or just to somehow "even the score" for the whole day.

Grandparents also can fall into the "mean teacher" trap. Their grandkids may learn to behave whenever Grandma threatens them or looks mad. As Grandma realizes this works, she may increase "looking (and acting) mad" to include most her family moments. Grandparents in this pitfall soon find that "looking mad" won't do, and they have to act "really mad." Now Grampa or Grandma have been pushed up a notch toward becoming behavior problems themselves!

So for Nancy and Martin to grow into happy, independent, productive adults, they need alternative activities to make the *"Let's-see-what-we-can-get-away-with"* game unimportant. When Grandma and Grampa are in charge of the kids, they should catch opportunities to encourage the kids. They also need to sharply limit punishment and use alternatives such as allowing the kids to make amends for mistakes as we do adults.

Carrying out all of this is more difficult and requires more planning than hard-headed Grampa's idea of *"thrashing it out of them."*

Reason #2: The Punishment Trigger is the Adult's Exasperation, Not the Child's Behavior.

In most situations with children, punishment is a dangerous practice partly because it may be more related to the frustrations and moods of the parent or grandparent in charge than to a child's mistakes.

Frequent use of punishment, when Grampa or Grandma have had it "up to here," usually results in a child more interested in the moment-to-moment mood of his grandparents than his own rights and wrongs.

So Grampa's punishment is also inconsistent because it will be related more to his frustrations and moods than to the grandkids' mistakes. If Grampa or Grandma use punishment when they have had it "up to here," Nancy and Martin will only be interested in that frustration point as the signal to ease up.

Reason #3: Punishment will be Imitated.

We usually think of a child's imitation of adults as very specific. *"Look at the way he walks, just like his Dad." "Look at the way she does her hair, trying to be just like her Mom."* But copying his parents or Grandma or Grampa is more likely to involve social habits. How does Grandma handle situations when things don't go right? What is Grampa's solution when others don't do what he wants? When Grampa is frustrated, how does he react? And how do Mom and Dad react in these situations?

We all know how quickly kids will pick up those words of frustration when Grampa hits himself on the kitchen drawer, but they also pick up the cues on *how to react* when things go wrong. Kids may get the message that the punishments, used by Grandma and Grampa, and maybe by Mom and Dad too, are good ways to deal with people.

The imitation of punishment may be included in the rest of your grandchild's social life. How should he handle friends when they don't do the "right thing?" A grandparent may become a role model for punishment. *"It works for Grandma, maybe it will work for me when I feel like it."* In any case, the most natural reflex to punishment is to give some back.

If it is not possible to punish his parent or grandparent, a child might turn to punishing others in his social circle.

So there's the possibility that a child will pick up some cues from your behavior about what is the appropriate reaction to unwanted behavior. If your granddaughter frequently criticizes and yells at her baby brother, a careful observation of her parents' or grandparents' own reactions might discover a clue as to where a daughter's reactions come from.

Children make a lot of mistakes--being led into errors by peers, forgetting chores and commitments, indulging in unhealthy foods and wasting time, to mention a few. When we see so many errors, we may find it difficult to be accepting and look at the long run. But the goal of teaching how to react to others may be more important than a mistake.

Reason #4: Punishment is Insulting, Belittling, and Lowers a Person's Self-Esteem

The emotional put-down of punishment distracts the victim from learning about the desired behavior. The punishment act, itself, is childish and belittles the significance of the victim. Isn't that why *adults* are so insulted when punishment is tried on them? So we all learn that the only possible ages for punishment are from two to about 18. Before that, it's called abuse; after that, it's hopeless.

Once a child's value of himself goes down, and the fear goes up, a new disadvantage develops for learning. Much of the childhood years are a trial-and-error process. The discoveries of "how to get along" come from a lot of guesses. How much guessing will a frightened person risk? Once your grandchild becomes discouraged and engaged in self-degrading thoughts, we all know learning will be slow.

In my college course in animal learning, students

have to teach their own pigeon to perform tasks by rewarding small successes. The first task is to get the pigeon to peck a disc by rewarding it with seeds, first for stepping toward the disc, followed by putting its head toward it, then touching it, and finally pecking it.

Sometimes students have trouble with the project because their pigeon is too scared to even move in its learning cage. If it had been handled roughly, or it had escaped and been chased down before being put in the learning cage, it may be too upset to do anything! Pigeons that won't do anything can't be taught anything. The student stares at the pigeon waiting for a chance to reward success. The pigeon stares at the student waiting for a chance to get out!

Punishment can produce the same impasse between grandchild and grandparent.

Reason #5: Punishment Encourages Stressful Behaviors.

Punishment will encourage bad habits such as nail-biting, hair-twirling and *"safer obsessions"* like video games and TV. These *"escapes"* are very stubborn habits maintained by their usefulness for avoiding contact with the punisher. Whenever encouragement and reward are low, these stress behaviors will increase. If the stressful behavior attracts some attention, then we are in a vicious cycle with a new long-term problem.

Reason #6: The Power Struggle.
Punishment will tempt a child to resist intimidation; the struggle takes over the family airways leaving little time for positive interactions and learning. A grandparent can "win" the power struggle, but, again, we have to have a loser.

The power struggle of punishment can spread to all family members. As others pick up the habit, a competition develops, *"Who can 'outdo'* (put down, criticize, reprimand, catch more mistakes of) *whom?"* It ruins the family as a nurturing place where learning is encouraged through practice—*with* mistakes.

Reason #7: Punishment is a Short-term Trap That Can Last Forever!
The bad habit of using punishment can be stubborn because it produces short-term results. For example, when Martin aggravates his Grandma Hazel, she may keep him in line by finding fault

where he is vulnerable, "*That music is terrible. Your hair is a mess! Your face is breaking out again.*"

With each of these insults, Martin's obnoxious behavior is temporarily interrupted while he defends himself, Grandma Hazel has released a little tension, and maybe Hazel has "taught Martin a lesson" or at least evened the score.

The long-term disadvantages of Grandma Hazel's punishment habit may go undetected because these problems will grow slowly. Martin will start the bad escape habits, he will feel worse about himself and about Grandma Hazel, and *he* will try to use punishment himself.

These two people are well on the way to a poor relationship where Martin annoys Grandma Hazel just to get even, and Grandma Hazel boils over now and then to gain temporary relief from her allergic reaction to him. Martin will learn when to let up a little, and he may also learn to imitate Hazel's insulting style just to gain more control.

Reason #8:   Discrimination.

A child subjected to a parent or relative in the "*I'll-get-even-with-you*" game learns the signals well. Innocent chaperones and teachers become fair game until they learn how to insult or scowl miserably enough to get control. An additional social problem is that no adult around a child like Martin likes to be forced to act mad or abusive and would rather avoid him, partly because they don't like the person they must become to keep control.

We all develop discriminations and act differently with different people. But when punishment is used, we do our best to avoid the punishing person altogether. The negative, critical, and threatening boss may have a reputation as a hard-liner, but the employees will duck and dodge her as much as possible. And they'll give no extra effort. Who wants to please her?

The relationship that develops is one in which two people only barely tolerate each other because they are forced to. A child may want to escape such a situation because of the possibility of being punished, and a parent or grandparent may want to be away (at work, at meetings, or just out anywhere) because of the uncomfortable reactions that seem to be called for at home.

Reason #9: When the Grandparents Take Care of the Kids, What Will They Find?

When Mom and Dad leave the kids with Grandma and Grampa, the grandparents may be left with the long-term side effects of punishments that were too severe and too frequent. A grandchild's solution may be to stop responding altogether or, at least, respond as little as possible. The situation has produced a kind of success, the child *is* quiet.

Even if the grandparents try a better approach later on, Nancy and Martin may refuse to risk coming out of their shells. The biggest wish of the kids is to get out—out of the room, out of sight, out of the house, if possible. Wouldn't we all rather dodge the punishment? With punishment you have to find your grandchild; with praise, your grandchild finds you.

As the experience is repeated, the situation preceding punishment signals a need to withdraw. The signal could be a classroom, a house, a time of day, a particularly dangerous person, or a combination of these. Once experiences have taught these signals, the mere termination of punishment is not likely to be immediately effective, because a child in these circumstances will be unwilling to take risks to find out if the danger has passed.

Many of the threats will very likely be of the one-shot nature. If they fail to produce results, Grampa may opt for larger punishments such as canceling a trip or party. Usually such one-shots (they usually only happen once or infrequently at most) are too late and produce the most resentment and argument with the least amount of change. Since parties and trips are infrequent, Grampa may feel he has to threaten a lot just to milk as much influence as possible from the upcoming event. Once the party or trip is over, he will have to dream up a new threat.

The one-shot leaves the person in charge with the dreary task of sorting out threats, bluffs, and final conclusions. In the process they are likely to fall into a negative reinforcement habit (see below).

Reason # 10: Punishments Can Lead to Divorce.

Any person being punished has one thought in mind, *"Get away!"* Children could plan running away or withdrawing if running away is impractical. And yet the conflict and confusion are intensified because their home is their most important source of security.

Whenever punishment is used, we are counting

on some other aspect of the situation to keep the child within range for deserved punishments. Either the doors must be locked, literally or figuratively, or the rewards from parents and grandparents are enough to overwhelm the unhappiness. One reason punishment strategies usually don't work on adults is that adults can leave.

2. Negative Reinforcement.

Isn't negative reinforcement the same as punishment? No, it's more subtle but also more common. The purpose of regular punishment, as everyone knows, is to reduce or eliminate bad behavior. Negative reinforcement is not punishment for mistakes, it's punishment for <u>failing</u> to do the right thing. The threat of a consequence for failing to meet someone's expectations is a common experience in a routine day.

Why do I make dinner for the kids at the same time every night, use their favorite plate, prepare only certain foods? Is it because the children watch for their chance to support my "good" behavior? No, the answer here usually begins, *"Well, if I didn't do that, the kids would complain and make a lot of trouble."*

When it is the *lack* of performance that produces bad consequences, it's called negative reinforcement. As long as I avoid unwanted dinner plates, unwanted food, delays, and don't disappoint my little masters, *I avoid* their nasty behavior.

The difference between regular punishment and negative reinforcement is important because the threat of negative reinforcement is always hounding the child or teenager. It has a continuous nature to it and, if not tested, the fear can continue long after the threat has passed.

Punishment in its consistent form, even with all its faults, is easy to understand: *"If I do the wrong thing, I'll get bad consequences."* Negative reinforcement has all the same faults as punishment with the added confusion of an obscure rule: *"If I fail to do the right thing, I'll get bad consequences."*

Grandma: *"Zac, did you pick up your clothes?"*

Zac: (Watching TV) *"Not yet."*

Grandma: *"Did you put your dirty clothes in the laundry?"*

Zac: *"No."*

Grandma: *"How about the mess in the living room?"*

Zac: *"OK, as soon as this is over."*

Grandma *"Take those dishes out, too."*

Zac: *"OK"* (Remains an intimate part of the couch.)

Grandma: (She's used no punishment so far, but now she reacts to Zac's *lack* of action.) *"Zac, I have had it! Now turn off that TV and get these things cleaned up!"*

Zac: *"OK, OK, don't have a cow about it."* (Mumbling) *"Gee, who knows when you're gonna blow up, anyway?"*

Grandma: *"What was that?"*

Zac: *"Nothing."*

Part of Zac's and Grandma's problem is that Grandma's strategy is the use of negative reinforcement. If Zac fails to perform (enough times), and Grandma asks him (enough times), then Grandma gets mad. Grandma may also support and compliment Zac if he cleans things up, but Grandma's exasperation limit and Zac's fear of her are the main factors at work in this situation.

At times, the distinction between punishment and negative reinforcement may seem like a word game. Could we simply say that Grandma threatens punishment for Zac's sloppiness? She could use that strategy—refuse to take him to a movie when he leaves his clothes all over, for example. But her reaction is negative reinforcement because it is triggered by the *lack* of behaviors and occurs at a non-specific time. Zac is tempted to continue to procrastinate, delay, and test the limits while Grandma is driven to using "mad" as a motivator.

Negative reinforcement does not produce a happy situation. If you do most of your activities everyday just to avoid someone's flack, you're probably unhappy with him or her (all spouses know who I'm talking about). *Positive* reinforcement is needed for a good relationship.

Grampa: *"Did you take the car in today?"*

Grandma: *"Yes, it just needed a tune-up."*

Grampa: *"Great, thanks for getting it done; that takes a lot off my mind."*

Grampa used the positive reinforcement idea, but in the next minute he slips to negative reinforcement:

Grampa: *"Did you get the little dinners I wanted for lunches?"*

Grandma: *"Didn't go by the store today."*

Grampa: *"Hey, I need a good lunch everyday."* (Here's a reprimand as negative reinforcement for Grandma's failure to do the right thing.)

Grandma: (Borrowing from Zac) *"OK, OK,*

don't have a cow over it. I'll get them tomorrow, and I'll make something good for you tomorrow."
(Mumbling) *"Gee, beam me up, Scotty!"*

Grampa: *"What was that?"*

Grandma: *"Nothing."*

Children have a better chance finding positive reinforcements everyday because parents, teachers, and grandparents know kids have to be encouraged. But negative reinforcement is probably the more common experience for us all even if it is a less popular term. It occurs when a behavior is used to <u>avoid</u> a consequence: Make your bed, or Grandma will be mad. Do your homework, or the teacher will embarrass you in front of the class. Keep your music low, or Grampa will be furious. Even though the intentions in these examples are to motivate, they sound like—and they are—threats.

The situation requires an effort to avoid the threatened outcome. A child might want to escape the situation altogether as with punishment. He could try to run away, but usually he will try to deal with it.

We're all familiar with the dark cloud of negative reinforcement produced by past bosses or parents, and the escape we, at times, wished for. We recognize it when we hear someone say, "Well, if

I didn't do it, I'd get so much flak..." If your day is filled with such efforts to stay out of the line of fire, you probably have leaving on your mind.

A marriage held together by one spouse hopping from one task to another trying to keep the other spouse from getting mad is an example. This unhappy situation may last for years, and it doesn't make a pleasant home environment either.

Even with the threat removed, a child (or spouse) may be afraid to risk ignoring an old threat, even when removed long ago. It will take some time and courage to test the new situation.

So here's a possible resolution: Every day, find something to compliment, appreciate, and support in all of those around you. Translate some old negative reinforcement into its flip side—the positive encouragement for what should be done instead of the criticism for failures. Gush a little, even if you have to be a little corny. Tell your grandchild you noticed when he makes a successful effort—cleaned up some dishes—said something nice to his brother—for example.

This "behavioral smile" is contagious; the kids are likely to copy your effort, and the new style will recycle through the family. Keep it up—even a spouse can pick up the habit!

Negative reinforcement in combination with an upcoming, one-shot event is a tempting strategy to try to get the kids to do right. *"If you don't stop complaining all the time, we'll just give up going to the beach this summer."* or, *"You had better show me you can get along with your brother, or I won't take you to the aquarium in town."* Because the threatened events happen only once or, very infrequently, they can't be a part of *repeated* practice—unless we add a lot of nagging, *"Remember what I said, treat your brother nice or no aquarium!"*

The threats for not acting right are negative reinforcement with all its bad baggage, so nagging sets in to milk the future one-shot event to get a little cooperation now.

Also, going to the beach is a singular future event not likely to be repeated for some time. Grandma and Grampa may repeat the *threat* many times since the vacation itself will only happen once. Of course, a child needs to learn that you mean what you say about the beach or about the aquarium, but the consequence is so far off that any outcome may seem unlikely.

So after all the argument, you either take the kid to the beach anyway, or you hold to your threat and don't take her/him. The first choice seems too lenient, but the second is too tough because it says that overall, he/she has been a bad kid. This one-shot consequence has no winners and little chance of a satisfactory outcome.

This situation is gloomy for the family and for the event when it finally comes. It's like holding off the enemy in battle with only one bullet; you have to do a lot of posturing, bluffing, and threatening. Once you use your bullet, you are an ogre for not allowing the beach or aquarium trip, or you are a patsy for giving in! And then the next time, you will need to threaten with a new bullet.

A better strategy is to allow yourself and your family the enjoyment of individual events without trying to use them to limit bad behavior or produce good behavior. Instead, choose some smaller event that can come up more frequently, something not so severe, that has a positive side to emphasize. For example, instead of threatening to withhold a birthday gift if semester grades don't come up (an unmanageable threat with an "only once" character to it), possibly each good grade on any test, quiz or paper could produce a trip to a local hangout for a tasty dessert. This procedure has the advantage of being a consistent and repeatable consequence while a grandparent emphasizes the right habits. It is not negative or severe, so we don't need to feel guilty and inconsistent. Coming from Grandma or Grampa, it provides more attention to the kids' success.

A very repeatable consequence makes it much easier to refrain from nagging. The repetition does the reminding. Nagging on the problem can stop, and the airways can be opened up for more pleasant family talk.

3. Why Would Anyone Use Punishment?

With all these discouraging problems, one might wonder why anyone would continue to use punishment. Even the choice of punishment should diminish when it is unsuccessful. So when a punishment doesn't get the desired result, why don't people change?

The answer is that in the very short term, punishment produces some results. If Grandma yells at Fred for using bad language, Grandma's punishment behavior may be reinforced by its immediate effect of interrupting Fred's bad behavior even if only temporarily. So Grandma is tempted to use it again.

Bad behavior seems to require a "quick-fix." Punishment may seem to fill the bill for children, but we seldom try it on adults. Instead, we use one of the following alternatives.

4. Five Alternatives to Punishment.

A large investment firm reneged on an announced $1.3 million dollar profit a few years ago because an accountant left off the minus sign—it was really a $1.3 million dollar *shortfall!* How did the firm's president discipline his accountant for the $2.6 million dollar mistake? To his disappointed stockholders he said, *"Well I guess that's why they put erasers on pencils!"* With adults, we usually get on with fixing the mistake. We deal with unwanted adult behavior every day, but like the accountant's president, most of us gave up punishment of the straightforward kind long ago.

The culture we live in continues to provide some punishment—"logical consequences" we sometimes call them—and the courts hand out jail sentences for the larger transgressions. But logical consequences and court sentences are usually long delayed and given only for repeated bad habits and big mistakes. So with unwanted *adult* behavior, what punishment alternatives do we use?

Every day, adult mistakes receive *very kind* reactions. Even blowing your horn at a poor driver's mistake is considered too aggressive. Often we just allow the person to make amends, or we ignore the mistake altogether. If we control the situation, we might try to make it less likely that he will repeat the mistake: *"The boss should give better instructions. He should put up more signs about how to use the printer!"* After more instruction, the boss may use warnings: *"Anyone caught putting their sandwich in the printer will be ... "* Then, if that doesn't work, maybe, punishment. Since punishment has so many disadvantages anyway, let's get on to a more adult way of handling problems.

Alternative #1:   Making Amends.

Making amends is the number one strategy adults use to handle bad adult behavior. If you come to my house for dinner tonight and spill your drink at the table, you don't expect me to threaten punishment by saying: *"Hey! What do you think you're doing? You're so clumsy! Now pay attention to what you're doing, or I'll send you home!"*

What nerve! Treating a guest like a child. What happened to "the benefit of the doubt?" You expect to be allowed to make amends; you expect me to belittle the problem, you even expect sympathy. *"Oh, too bad. No problem, I'll get a cloth."* You say, *"I'm sorry, let me get that. I'll take care of it."*

Isn't adulthood nice? Even with big mistakes, we would rather have the offender try to fix the mistake than punish him. At what age did you, and our innocent accountant with the 2.6 million dollar mistake, earn such consideration? Why wasn't *he* punished? Because it wouldn't help, and it would look as if the investment firm was a simple-minded company, naive and heartless. After all, mistakes happen.

Two-year-olds, teenagers, and accountants who make mistakes, accidental or not, should be allowed to make amends. Not that our accountant could make up for his mistake in this century. Your grandchildren deserve the same respect. It is only fair to assume they are doing their best.

Remember the movie about a troublesome city teenager whose life was popping with mistakes that he could never see coming? His parents punished him, hoping he would avoid future "accidents." At last, in exasperation they sent him to the country farm to live with his grandparents. We saw our teenager toil the whole afternoon, making amends for a clumsy mistake, spilling the milk can, then cleaning up the spill. Finally finished, he went into dinner, justified, un-criticized, and with an experience that motivated him to be more careful.

At home he would have been restricted or physically punished and belittled, and he would have lost the practice of making things right. Though the movie lesson was unrealistically easy and quick, the message was a good one: our teenager learned by making amends and cleared up his guilt; and the adults maintained a healthier relationship with him in the bargain.

Mom: (Sitting down to dinner) *"Whoops, now I know what I forgot at the store—coffee! But we have juice, how about that?"*

Grandma: *"Don't worry about it; juice is fine."* (Grandma belittles the mistake)

Mom: *"At least I'll get out the juice."* (Mom makes amends)

Nancy: *"I accidentally erased our list of names and addresses from the computer today."*

Mom: *"What! Didn't you put it back from the flash drive? I was looking for that for half an hour this afternoon. You're so inconsiderate at times. Don't you have enough sense to..."*

Grandma: (Interrupting) *"Nancy, after dinner, find the right flash drive and reload the address file, OK?"* (And then to Mom) *"I can get along without the coffee if you can, so don't worry about it."*

Mom: *"What? Oh, ah, yes, OK, OK. If I get a break on forgetting the coffee, I guess Nancy gets a break, too. And, Nancy, could you add the names on the outside of my phone book?"*

Alternative #2:   Ignoring.

Ignoring behavior eventually decreases it, especially if our child was acting up to get attention. If a grandparent can tough it out and hold back attention for bad language, our child may go on to something more acceptable. The problem here is that in the short-run, *more bad behavior* is likely rather than less. This bad behavior has been a part of a habit to get some entertainment or attention from Grandma and Grampa. Now they plan to cut that off. For example, no more attention for bad language.

If the usual amount of swearing will no longer

work, what should our child do? He may escalate the volume, frequency, or foulness of the talk. At the "higher" level, his grandparents may break the new rule and punish this outrageous behavior. If that quiets things down, grandparents may return to the ignoring rule only to go back to punishment when the assault on the ears again reaches pain threshold. The process builds up a new level of bad behavior. Escalation is a very common problem because the natural childish reaction to failure (to get attention) is escalation.

Ignoring means consistently overlooking relatively unimportant, undesirable behaviors and paying attention to other aspects of a child's actions. When Tim shaved his hair nearly to the middle of his head, his parents felt it was within his personal grooming choices to do so, but when he slapped his younger sister, they reacted strongly. Their different reactions to these very different behaviors keep the priorities straight and reduce unnecessary criticism.

Alternative #3: Adding Something Good to the Ignoring Plan.

Grandma and Grampa need to have a plan to encourage good behaviors and be alert to the first opportunity to work the plan! Ignoring the unwanted behavior *and* planning to encourage *specific, likely,* good behaviors will produce better results. The message needs to be clear: *"Now that's a good way to handle that." "I liked hearing about your report on the Civil War battle. You're learning about interesting things." "I noticed you helped clear the table after supper. That was great!"*

"Catch 'em being good" means recognize, praise, or reward the good behavior you see. Perhaps you remember as a child thinking: *"When I make mistakes everyone notices, and I get in trouble, but a lot of times I do well, and nobody says anything."*

To prevent unwanted behaviors, grandparents need to "catch 'em being good," not just when the desired behavior occurs, but when a behavior in the right direction comes along. Actions that are improvements and a step forward need the most encouragement, recognition, praise and reward.

Research tells us that catching people when they come near to appropriate behavior is a more efficient learning technique than punishment for errors. Considering all the possibilities for error, a child isn't much closer to learning an important skill just by being told, *"Wrong!"*

Alternative #4: Using the Cost of Inconvenience.

Many little inconveniences may seem trivial, at first, but when put into practice they may be extremely effective. For example, if Grampa has to put a penny in a jar on the kitchen table every time he loses his temper, it may seem like a trivial act for someone with plenty of pennies. But if the rule is strictly followed, the inconvenience of having to stop, get a penny, go into the kitchen and put it in the jar can be a very effective consequence. Pennies are unimportant, but the behavioral "cost" makes this consequence work.

Many psychologists use the principle of inconvenience as a strategy for removing or reducing smoking in adults. The heavy smoker is instructed to keep an exact record of his smoking throughout each day. He carries a little notebook wherever he goes and writes down the time, to the minute, when he takes out a cigarette, and the time he puts it out. He may be asked to note the situation as well, including who was with him, and what he was doing. Some psychologists also ask for the cigarette butts to be saved and brought in for counting. These tasks may not seem like consequences as we have discussed them so far, but they are consequences of a most useful type. They cost time, and many a smoker is just too busy to make all those entries and save butts, so he takes a pass on having the next cigarette.

Such a self-administered procedure requires a very cooperative and trustworthy subject. I have found the cost-of-inconvenience procedure useful when smokers referred to me have been told by their doctor that their health or even their life is at stake! They usually *want* the process to work, and they can be counted on to cooperate. The procedure has not worked well with people who *"feel they should cut down."* With these less motivated subjects, it takes a stronger procedure than raising the cost of inconvenience.

Sometimes teenagers can be enthusiastic about a record-keeping procedure. One mother told me her 19-year-old son, Damon, continually disrupted the family by "checking things." On some evenings, he insisted on checking as many as 70 things before going to bed. Damon checked to see if the back door was locked. He checked to see if the light was out in the basement. He checked to see if his pen was on his desk, and if his dresser drawers were completely closed. Some of this would have been reasonable, but the situation got out of hand when he checked the same thing for the fifth or sixth time in the same evening.

At first his checking was examined for the possibility that it was an attention-getting behavior. Some progress was made by reducing Damon's parents' attention to the excessive checking and increasing conversation time before he went off to bed. The most effective procedure was beginning a record of every item checked, the time it was checked, the result of the check, and what could have happened if the item had been left unchecked and undone. The procedure involved so much writing and decision-making that it was nearly impossible to check 70 things each evening.

Because of the work and inconvenience of the procedure, Damon began to pass up items that were not so important, and he made a special effort to remember the ones already checked, or he looked at his record, so that he didn't have to do it again! The number of times Damon checked things soon was down to a level that was only a little unusual instead of disruptive to the family.

The same principle of inconvenience can be used to increase a habit. For example, good homework habits can be influenced by how convenient it is to get started. If there is a place to do homework with little distraction that is well supplied with paper and such, then we have a better chance of getting some homework done.

Alternative #5: Consequences, Even Time-outs, Must Give Way to Modeling.

Sometimes the bad behavior demands a reaction. We don't let adults get away with just anything and children becoming adults shouldn't be misled that anything goes either. What alternative is there when bad behavior should not be ignored, and making amends or hoping for opportunities for encouragement is not enough?

For young children, time-out is often a good solution but may not be appropriate for older children. We all know the drill of putting a child on a chair, or in his/her room for older ones, for a little "cooling off" as a kind of punishment. The procedure can work well if the threats, arguments, and other verbal decorations that often precede the time-out are kept to a minimum.

Grampa: (after Liz throws a toy at her sister.) *"Liz! We don't throw toys. You could hurt someone. That's One!"* (Liz throws again.) *"Liz, I told you,* that's _Two_"

    Liz: *"I don't want it!"* (Liz throws again.)

    Grampa: *"OK, that's Three,"* Grampa takes Liz to the kitchen chair and deposits her there.

    Grampa is doing well with the younger one. He doesn't talk much during the count which could lead Liz to act up more; he doesn't make a lot of threats; and he corrects the behavior in a way that can be used frequently—no dramatic punishment that requires a big build-up.

    Time-out for young children means spending a short time in a quiet place, alone, after inappropriate behavior. It can be very successful. The separation of younger children from others interrupts overheated verbal and physical reactions with a calming-down period. When your grandchild regains emotional control, she or he can discuss what happened and plan changes.

    The time period that is most helpful is long enough to break up unwanted behavior and tempers, but short enough for everyone to remember clearly what happened and want to plan other reactions. Just having time-out for a minute or two is effective; a long time-out is not necessary nor helpful.

    This alternative cuts off fighting between

siblings and helps a parent or grandparent regain perspective and control, instead of escalating a problem situation. Time-out may prevent physical and verbal punishments that are regretted later.

Punishment frequently prevents discussion and planning for changes. Because of bad feelings, the bad behavior is likely to occur again. But after time-out, each person involved in the problem has a chance to tell his/her feelings and make suggestions. Everyone can practice listening and understanding and gain experience planning for a change. Time-out sets the stage for a new beginning.

When Grandma returned from shopping, she noticed lipstick on the kitchen wall. Mike had been talking on the phone instead of watching his younger sister, Tina, the wall artist.

Mike: *"But I have to talk on the phone to my friends sometimes. It drives me crazy to watch Tina every minute. I shouldn't have to watch her this much! How could she do that? I'm not going to clean that up. I have to leave to go to the mall with Bill."*

Grandma: *"We're going to have to talk about this now."*

Mike: *"I can't stand it! It's not my faul. Tina should have to clean it up! Grandma, you can't make me do this."*

Grandma: *"Mike, I'm getting mad, and you're upset too. Cool off for five minutes in your room, and then we'll put our heads together to work this out."* (Mike stomps out to his room.)

When the two get together after cooling down, it's more likely they will be able to make a compromise. Perhaps Grandma, Mike, and Tina can do the wall cleaning together. The baby-sitting needs more planning and incentives. Mike needs some specific activities to do with Tina while baby-sitting, and he can be given extra time with his friends for doing a good job. When you try to reach a solution, if either you or your grandchild find you can't be reasonable, extend the time-out until all persons can contribute to the agreement.

For a child who is almost an adult, the time-out method will seem more and more childish. After all, except for long time-outs in prisons, you seldom see it used in the adult world. Your example, on the other hand, will always be an influence on grandchildren even in the decades to come.

Grandparents have a special and important role

in passing on family traditions and standards that can help a young person keep direction. Grandma said, *"In the Weiler family we try to think and respect everyone in the family <u>and</u> outside of it. I expect you to live up to the Weiler standard."* Of course, Grandma's actions must follow her words. Family sayings pass along meaningful values for the whole family. My father was fond of saying, *"With all thy getting, get understanding."*

The following examples I have heard show how modeling and positive consequences work together. A grampa who wanted a child to read books turned off the TV and began reading an exciting adventure novel aloud with his grandson. A grandmother who wants her granddaughter to be honest can ask, *"Whose money is this under the kitchen table?"* instead of just pocketing it. When a grandfather noticed shoes accumulating by the front door, he put his in the closet, and soon his grandson's shoes were not at the front door either. The power of what we do is surprising; it's natural for members of the family to observe and be affected by it. Imitation occurs every day.

I worked with a teenager who had a problem controlling anger. He started fights when classmates teased him and he felt bad about himself later. His parents as well as his grandparents needed to demonstrate and describe their methods of controlling anger in their lives.

Grandma shared a story: *"I was driving to the post office today, and when I changed lanes, another driver honked a long time at me. I guess he thought I slowed him down. I felt mad and thought about pulling over and shaking my fist at him. But I said to myself, 'I'm angry, but I'm in control—not him. I'm not going to let him make me do something dangerous.'"* Sharing family experiences is an important part of modeling.

Allowing a child to make amends, using time-outs, ignoring some things, looking for something good, *all* require diligent effort. Contrary to the easy, and sometimes magical, advice from aunts, uncles, some professionals, and even some grandparents, being a parent or grandparent can be downright hard work. So make sure you eliminate rules about trivial behaviors before you start any of these plans.

Suggestion 5: Help with the "Boy Problem" and School Work

For every 100 male college graduates there are over 140 women graduates.

1. The "Boy Problem."

Boys are five times more likely than girls to have accidents with bikes, sticks and baseball bats. Later on, they are four times more likely to have trouble with the law. During the teenage years, U.S. boys cause most driving accidents and get most of the traffic tickets. They also have lower grades in school and are more likely to drop out. Boys have shrunk to a minority in colleges, medical schools, and law schools. Although girls were rarely even allowed in these institutions little more than a century ago, now, for every 100 male college graduates there are now over 140 women graduates.

The Southern Regional Education Board studied 40,000 typical high school students, not stars and not low performers, in 2002. While 84 percent of girls said it was important to continue schooling after high school, only 67 percent of boys agreed.

The genders are different, and there is a "Boy Problem."

Now that the "male chores" of the farms of 1900 have become less needed, girls have an advantage. Girls make an earlier contribution to the family, particularly in the domestic chores. As a result, they enjoy early appreciation and are better prepared to care for themselves.

Grandparents tend to cave in to flack from boys while resisting any flack from girls. With insistence on girls doing their chores and homework, the girls develop skills faster then their brothers. Boys may receive less encouragement from exasperated parents or because boys dodge the work altogether, and they fall further behind in the experience department.

Granddads are particularly vulnerable to competition with their grandsons and hold back on compliments for chores well done for fear of appearing weak.

Grandparents can support the school's active projects in home improvement, financial management, small business management, mortgages, stock markets, computer management, applied science, and tracking diet and exercise. These projects encourage both boys and girls to be proud of their abilities right now. This pays off for both parents and grandparents as the kids (particularly the boys) build self-esteem and competencies. "I'm not 'just a kid,' I can do things." Even abstract subjects can include practical applications at home.

College applications may not ask about these "non-academic" skills, but schoolwork should help children with concerns now, at their present age. "Someday you'll need this," is not enough. They need a good answer to, "What good is this (homework, project, learning, work) now?" You can help their parents provide answers.

Going from father to grandfather, I went from girls who have the highest grades in school and are the least likely to need school discipline, to boys who are most likely to be disciplined and six times more likely to have trouble with the law, with driving, with alcohol and drugs, and six times more likely to go to prison later on.

Is all this genetic? Some of it must be but there are positive, and negative, contributing factors from parents and grandparents.

Many parents, teachers, and counselors believe

girls are more socially skilled at an earlier age and therefore may attract more support, acceptance, and admiration than their brothers. Boys on the other hand, seem to want only to be competent and be admired for it. They seem to shun the gushier praise. To prove they are not easily influenced, boys often fend off sincere praise in the years when they need it most.

The lack of enthusiasm from a grandson may lead Grampa to conclude that compliments and admiration don't work, so he should lay off the positive approach. This is a deadly mistake.

Neither Grampas nor Grandmas should be misled by short-term rebuffs because the long-term results are more important. The temptation to let boys go their own way, with discipline for only the big blunders and a trickle of support for the successes, is destructive to skill development in boys.

While "protecting" a boy from drudgery, parents can run the risk of driving their son to look for other activities that show he can "do something," Can Grandma help?

Threatened by his perceived "worthlessness," a boy might cast around for a way to show off—what will he find? Will it be a suggestion from his parents or grandparents? Or will encouragement from friends make risky behaviors more likely?

Positive support is the major advantage parents and grandparents have in competing against friends of their children who encourage and criticize without much thought.

One fast way to alienate a member from a group (or family) is to deny him a chance to contribute when he's ready. Gripe as a grandson may about chore assignments and household jobs, recognition of his step forward now will help maintain his genuine satisfaction with himself later on when peers encourage dangerous habits.

Projects in home improvement, cooking, financial management, small business management, mortgages, stock markets, setting up a new cell phone and tracking diet and exercise all encourage boys as well as girls to be proud of their abilities right now. Even abstract subjects can include practical projects. Talk to your grandchildren about the skills and knowledge you use everyday.

2. Who is Gifted?

Soccer and basketball coaches are not the

only adults putting kids to the test and seeking the stars. The schools are forever testing our children, looking for the "gifted." They do it because they have special programs for special kids. And some of us want "trophy children." But how would a parent recognize, and how should a grandparent react to, a child's "gifts?"

Who were the geniuses of the past? Einstein, for sure, even though his genius wasn't detected until he was nearly an adult. Many people would include Mozart who was writing operas at the age of three. But the musical genius of Mozart or Michael Jackson did not guarantee a long and happy life.

We might include others in math and theoretical physics, as well as additional nominations from the list of classical composers. No doubt these people were born with something special. Einstein even left his brain to science, so they could try to figure out what it was—they have never offered any conclusions.

Grandparents have a special role here: paying attention to all their grandchild's interest and abilities. Giving encouragement and praise is a grandparent's most important job.

The long-term Adolescent Health Study shows

that the kids most likely to get into self-destructive activities such as drinking, drugs, or crime are kids who do poorly in school.

The study has been following 12,000 students since 1994 when they were 12 to 17 years old. It found all the familiar problems you would expect. At first, one in ten reported weekly drinking, and the amount of sexual behavior was alarming. One in five seventh and eighth graders had explored sexual activities, and two out of three high school juniors and seniors were sexually experienced. I doubt the statistics are any better, now.

After problems with school, the second best predictor of these bad habits was the amount of unsupervised time these teenagers ordinarily had. This influence showed up in drug use, violent behavior, and sex. "Among all the factors that can be associated with teenage sex, the big one was opportunity," Dr. Robert Blum, the director of the study, said.

We seem to have adjusted to a daily routine that says, "Get the children up before it's light; get them to school by 7:45 ready or not; and dismissed from school by 2:00." To do what? Even a large proportion of adults have trouble being bright morning people.

This goes double for teenagers going through the growth and hormone years.

Since after-school time is such a factor in risky and violent behaviors, maybe we should reorganize high school schedules. When classes begin at 7:45, teens may go home soon after lunch to an empty house and three hours of unsupervised time before parents get home from work.

What sense is there in going to math class at 7:45 a.m. in a sleepy haze and going to football practice at your afternoon peak? It should be math at your peak and sports when they can be worked in.

Grandparents with a little free time and transportation might want to help out here, offering to give the grandkids a ride home from school, plan an after-school activity or just be there when the grandkids come home from school.

3. Bullies, Victims and Hiding Out in School.

Every school day, 160,000 students will stay home because of bullies, the U. S. Department of Justice estimates. Also, 100,000 students will bring guns to school, 6,500 teachers will be threatened, and 250 teachers will be attacked—every day.

Bullies often justify their aggression by saying

they were provoked, and the victims deserved mistreatment because they didn't comply with the bully's demands. Bullies like to dominate others and think they should always get their way.

Girl bullies may sometimes use more subtle tactics than their more violent brothers, such as insults and ridicule, but the terror they inflict can still be intense and cruel. So victims avoid unsupervised areas, restrooms, recreation areas, the lunchroom or Face Book just to keep from being the repeated targets.

Victims of bullies can be passive or provocative. Passive victims are often alone, anxious, sometimes weaker, and may cry easily. Provocative victims can bring trouble on themselves because they tease and irritate others and don't know when to back off. When they get an unwanted reaction, they sometimes fight back, but usually ineffectually.

What can a parent, a grandparent, or teacher do? The single most effective deterrent to bullying is an adult authority. Adults should intervene. We can do it with a no-nonsense style, as a problem solver and as a third person who smoothes things over.

In the cafeteria, Taylor, who is 14 and has been the subject of many bullying complaints, shakes his fist at Richard and says, "You'd better hand over that quarter left from your lunch."

Ms. Anderson, the social studies teacher, overhears and says, "Taylor, that doesn't go here. Come to my room for the rest of your lunch time—we need to talk." (The no-nonsense and prompt action approach.)

"No-Bullying Rules" and school policies that encourage students to speak out and get adult help when needed should be supported by parents and grandparents. Our goal should be to protect the victims and to help the bully replace negative behaviors with skills that involve treating others kindly.

This problem requires a statement right from the top. School superintendents should assure principals, and principals should assure teachers, that they will be vigorously supported in their efforts to stop bullying in the school and out of school.

Signs of bullied students:
- Making excuses for not wanting to go to school.
- Increased fear of school situations such as riding the bus, going outside or using the

restroom.
- Missing personal items or needing extra school supplies or money.
- Extra trips to the school nurse, unexplained bruises or torn clothing.

All of us are aware of the consequences of bullying. Kids will be hiding out in school and losing out on their education while they try to stay out of harm's way. "If I don't go to the bathroom (gym, school bus, outside areas, or lunchroom), I can avoid Billy (or Beth) Bully for another day."

Teachers and principals deserve your support. And many children need special practice learning how to talk firm, walk tall, look a tormentor in the eye and say loudly, "Back off!" As city police often tell us, some people need to practice with how to avoid looking and acting like a victim.

The bullies also need help. They, too, are missing out on their education while their attention is diverted to confronting, fighting, and abusing.

They will soon be out of school with minimal social skills and the mistaken notion that abusing others is acceptable. They need redirection.

Let's help them now while they are in school,

and teachers and staff have an influence.

The person who brings the problem to our attention is often denounced as a "tattletale." One reason tattletales annoy us is that the help requested is not easy or comfortable. In some cases, it's dangerous. The bully may retaliate, or the bully's parents may object to our interference.

Our freedom and safety exist only because most people will not tolerate behavior that endangers others. If we saw thugs beating up someone, we'd yell for help or call the police. We wouldn't expect the police to say the victim should "solve his own problem." And we would not expect to be ridiculed as a "tattletale."

Bullies at school are a local example of a weakening of the majority's will to protect the individual. Tattletales are not admired, and neither are bullies. School policies should encourage students to object when one of their own is bullied by another. And teachers should support reasonable requests for help. Tattletales are not always wrong.

School psychologist Izzy Kalman offers direct help for the kids with a online manual, *How to Stop Being Teased and Bullied Without Really Trying*. His website, www.bullies2buddies.com also has a free manual and advice for adults.

The rewards for teasing and bullying are in the reactions of the victim, says Kalman. He makes specific suggestions in his manuals and CDs about how a child should react or not react. In fact, he contends the cure for bullied victims is to learn new reactions to the bullies.

The bullies of today will be the community problems of tomorrow. From their ranks will come the next generation of child abusers, spouse abusers, road-rage, and "life rage".

4. Magical Thinking and Mental Habits.

The signers of the Declaration of Independence knew the value of both education and hard work. It was clear to them that effort and learning in school would be rewarded in work and life.

Today, many students believe they might "make it" even to enormous financial success just by luck, or by skill in sports or music, or by knowing the right people in the entertainment business. It's a possibility promoted by TV, news, and state lotteries.

So without incentives to focus attention on the learning at hand, many students become victims of magical thinking about success, and they develop unrealistic views of how "luck" will carry them through.

We adults also become victims of magical thinking. That's why we now approve of lotteries and other gambling, but our grandparents wisely, I think, did not.

We sometimes engage in magical thinking not only about a financial windfall, but also about our students: *"The ones with the 'right stuff' will always do well." "Kids will work harder at school if parents take a harder (more punitive) line or if the teachers enforce strict (more punitive) rules."*

Faced with a student's failure and rebellion, a parent is tempted to criticize and punish. But the solution is on the positive side—with incentives, praise and respect expressed in concrete ways that raise self-esteem and confidence.

Some may object that gushing with praise is the wrong suggestion, but the danger for most of us isn't in overdoing it, but in doing it at all. Encouragement and parental (and grandparental) support involve a commitment of time and attention.

But schools are crowded, teachers are busy, and our culture is inclined to provide little compensation for the essential activities of attending school and learning.

Representatives in Congress with their large salaries and teachers on the line with their modest ones should pause before objecting to the notion of rewarding students. It may be the most important part of the teaching and the parenting job. Few of us work for nothing.

I know it seems like a lot of trouble, and we wish all students would work just for the joy of it and learn just for the love of learning, but most will not. We are a goal-oriented species with ambitions that can go astray. We need daily course corrections through positive feedback.

If a student behaves badly in school, we often say it is his fault—he is rebellious, aggressive, too distracted, or not very smart. In a well-known study focused on how we explain children's problems, school psychologists listed the following causes of school problems:

1. The material was not appropriate,
2. The teacher was not doing a good job of teaching,
3. The organization of the school was wrong,
4. The parents of the student were not supportive,

5. Something about the student was amiss—lack of motivation, low ability, or emotional disturbance.

When teachers were asked to think back about the students they had taught, they attributed 85 percent of the problems to No. 5, the students themselves. This is partly true, of course, but it attributes the problem to the factor that is most difficult to change.

All of us can also engage in the faulty mental habit of blaming a person's basic personality. This can get in the way of resolving problems. As a grandparent you can bolster successes with encouragements and compliments which will produce the best long-term progress. Knowing the pitfalls of blaming the child's personality can clear the way to a better attitude and a better solution. Here are a few versions of faulty blaming habits that can sometimes afflict everyone in the family.

1. Oversimplification.

We are all inclined to simplify to keep order in our mind. Some disorder is inherent, but the habit is destructive.

All those teachers are mean."

"Well, if you would just try a little harder, I'm sure things would get better."

You can see that oversimplification can be both a grandparent's and a child's problem. A good step forward in this conversation would be to ask a specific question instead of keeping the focus on the child's bad behavior, *"What would show your teachers your good side?"* Of course, this question won't get a direct and constructive answer, but it will turn the topic toward more productive advice than "<u>you</u> should try harder."

2. Absolutes.

We prefer absolutes. Gray areas and contradictions are too hard to handle while an absolute demand seems more likely to get results.

Faced with an absolute demand, *"I want all your homework done before supper, not a bit left or no TV later,"* a child-teen may react with his own no-room-for-argument tactic, *"Either you love me or you don't. If you loved me, you would let me do it when I want to, so I guess you don't love me."*

Grandma could make better progress here by setting a reachable goal, *"If you have the writing part done before supper, you can do the math after your program."* This suggestion won't stop the arguing, but it is more likely to reach a solution.

3. I'll make them sorry.

"I just won't do her stupid project; that'll fix her."

"Mark, giving up won't hurt your teacher; it will only prolong the problem, and it will lower your grade." Mark dreams of his power over the teacher, but Grandma has to help him be realistic.

4. Everyone is watching me.

"My hair looks terrible, and everyone will notice this shirt is crummy and faded."

Grandma can help here by giving her granddaughter a broader view: *"Lisa, what were Althea and Margery wearing last Tuesday?"*

"Grandma, how would I know?"

"People don't pay much attention, do they? The same goes for Althea and Lisa."

We all want the best for our children and that's why we are tempted to point out the shortfalls, but it's the example you put in front of them—even the mental habit you show—that has the most impact. A discussion of all sides of the problem will produce the most useful conclusion.

As their grandchildren reach their early teens, some grandparents are surprised at how much guidance and practice their young teenagers need. School and friends begin taking up the largest amount of a teen's time and attention and just a little coaching from grandparents can be a long-lasting help for a teen struggling to adjust to everything at once.

Adults looking back realize that school success was a critical ingredient of happiness in our childhood and teenage years. If you can help your grandteen in this important part of his or her life, what a gift it is! And that success provides more than confidence in academic abilities, it influences feelings of competence and usefulness outside of school as well.

Looking back again, we grandparents remember how we compared ourselves to schoolmates and reached an impression of them and a judgment of ourselves as well—possibly before we were 10, but certainly during our teenage years. Grandparents who have attended their school reunions know how the reunion seems to measure us against that old bench mark again. This common reaction to reunions demonstrates how important help in school is to your student.

School is such a large part of a child's life, and if it isn't going well, it clouds almost all other activities.

Suggestion 6: Helping Your Grandchild Make Friends

How can you say, "I like you"?

A crucial growing-up question is, *"Grandma, how can I get along with the other kids?*

Of course there are no quick-fix answers, but a grandparent can pass along rules of conversation and a little advice about being interested in other people.

Brian: *"So, Greg, how did your soccer game go?"*

Greg: *"What? Oh, it was OK."*

Brian: *"Must have been a mess with all that rain."*

Greg: *"Yeah, you should have seen the mud near the goal; our goalie looked like a pig!"*

Brian: *"Our field still had some grass down there."*

Greg: *"Did you have to play that Kickers team?"*

Brian: *"Yes, have you played them yet?"*

Brian has a good social habit of an occasional question. Most adults learn early that part of getting along is remembering to express some genuine unselfish interest in other people.

1. How Do You Like Your Grandchildren?

Occasionally, I am invited to talk at a local school's PTA, and I often begin with this question, "How many of you folks love your children?" My audience usually thinks this is a peculiar question but after some hesitation, most raise their hands. Then I say, "Here's a similar question, how many of you <u>like</u> them?" Now the hesitations are longer, but many finally raise their hands. Some may even volunteer, "I love them, but I just don't always like what they do."

With some discussion, we often agree that love is about our basic attitude toward someone, but liking is about individual behaviors.

Many grandparents tell their grandchildren they love them frequently, but they say "I like you" much less often. And many children can be cynical and believe that being "likable" is different. They think it's an "inborn" characteristic, and each of us must suffer with our inherited "personality." But most adults have seen a low responder like Greg "brighten up" or "turn around" with a compliment or question that shows interest in his life. How responsive and "attractive" Greg is can change. It depends on his companions and his own effort.

Brian's attractive habit is often imitated, and Greg, who is not usually outgoing, picks up the topic and finally has a question of his own about "that Kickers team." Brian partly creates his own pleasant social world. Both Brian and Greg probably like each other because of the reactions they "draw out" of each other.

2. "Likable" is More than Asking Questions.

Some kids are likable for reasons way beyond appearance and "personality." We parents and grandparents know that being "likable" is also made up of specific behaviors; it's a matter of *showing* some genuine unselfish *liking* of others— not by overusing those words, "I like you," but by approving, praising or agreeing with particular remarks or behaviors. People with this attractive habit are not only likable, but they are also often imitated. Therefore, they create more attractive behavior in the people around them.

Just asking a few questions, as Brian does, will not turn a person's social life around. He will need to make other efforts as well. And he may still believe that appearance is first on the *"Likable Characteristics List"* and that saying clever, cool, or funny remarks is second. But Brian has learned the liking principle, a characteristic that is missing from the list, but it shows up when our grandson is asked who *he* likes. Usually, the answer is that he likes people who accept him, admire him, and want to spend time with *him*!

Sometimes the view from the other person's perspective leads to the discovery that: *"To be liked, I should watch out for being too critical and make an effort to like others."* This would include habits of asking about the other person but would also include showing concern, complimenting, expressing agreement instead of criticism, and paying attention to the listening tips of Suggestion 1.

One Grandma described the difference between her granddaughters to me this way: *"Dianne and her sister Kelly are so different! Kelly can't stop talking, and Dianne hardly says a word. It's hard to believe they were raised in the same family!*

"Last week, I picked them up from a

neighborhood party, and when I asked them how it went, Kelly said, 'It was great! They dropped all these balloons on us and everyone screamed! Sally was there, Ann was there, Betty, Millie, and all the boys, Frank, Donald, David and Chris.'"

When Grandma asked Dianne how it went she just said, *"It was OK. Everyone was acting silly."* But Kelly said Dianne just stood around.

Being sociable is like many other activities: If you're good at it, you like it, and you tend to practice more of it. On the other hand, if you don't get started with others easily, you will have a little less practice, and the cycle continues.

Kelly's focus is on others; she asks a lot of questions and remembers a lot of details about others that she is forever talking about. Dianne's concern is for her own security. She can't seem to think of anything safe to say.

Both girls have habits that perpetuate their attitudes. Kelly talks a great deal, she is loud, and she has learned about the other kids. Dianne doesn't talk much, she uses a soft voice, and her lack of experience with the others leaves her short on subjects to bring up.

Dianne doesn't have a "problem." She has a

quiet style which sometimes makes her feel left out, but she shouldn't be given the extra burden of being told she has something wrong with her.

Her parents could give her extra social ammunition before she goes into a social situation. Adults help each other with this kind of priming quite often: *"Remember* (Grandma says on the way to her office party with Grampa) *my boss, Jane, has a boat out on the town lake, and she just got back from Florida. Tom bought a car like ours and Bob Teak's daughter recently made him a grandfather."*

These little bits of information will allow Grampa to *"go more than half way"* in starting a talk with Grandma's co-workers—if he wants to.

Dianne needs some help with information too. She may complain that *"No one came over to me at the party,"* but the parental reflex of *"Did you go over to any of them?"* could be left off while providing whatever information might be helpful to Dianne in thinking up something to start a conversation.

Grampa doesn't get a lecture on how to correct some defect in himself on the way to Grandma's party, he's just provided with a better chance of doing what he wants to do with information about the others. And Dianne doesn't need more criticism either, just some long-term help as the situations come up, so that if she is inclined to join in the talk, the detail of thinking of a topic will be easier.

A person who is good at socializing has many friends; they laugh at the same things and cooperate on the same tasks. They don't seem to try to please each other, they just do. The notion of being pleasing in order to get along with others may seem a little simple-minded and of little use until pleasing, agreeing, disagreeing, fighting, and cooperating are seen as special cases of social rewards and mild punishments.

Most children worry about how attractive or likable they are and certainly some primping before an outing can make a difference. However, like adults, *they* think their attractiveness is largely based on their physical appearance while their judgment of others largely depends on what the others *do*! So it follows that in order to be likable, children will have to do some liking.

Cool, moody, critical, sarcastic, angry, or bitter people make interesting characters in movies. In real life, such characters are not well-liked because they rarely show genuine interest in others.

3. Liking and Caring Behaviors are Attractive.

Do your family members use liking behaviors? If so, then preparing for an outing will not be a stressful time for your grandchild because he/she understands the basics that make a person likable. The moments before a party can be planning time: *"At the party I want to spend time with . . . I want to talk to . . . I will show I like (fill in the blank) by . . ."*

Natural liking behaviors are consistent attention, questions, encouragement, and praise, instead of preoccupation with your own looks and interests. If you do more asking and listening than you do telling, then you're probably on the right track. Liking behaviors are habits that grow with practice and replace their opposites—silence or criticism, sarcasm, and negative comments.

Answers are impressive, but questions send the messages. A teen asks about her boyfriend's studying; he asks about her day. The messages show concern—they say, *"I'm interested in you."*

In marital counseling a common assignment for both members of the couple is to have "caring days"—days when he or she does a particular thing for his or her spouse—without being asked or expecting anything in return. What do you suppose is the request most often listed for the caring day by the wife? She says, *"I wish he would ask me about my day sometimes."* Out of all the things a husband could say, this simple wish is the most common request: personalized interest and attention.

Liking is not always returned, and two-way relationships will not balance exactly. One person will be required to go more than half-way to make it work. Socially successful and likable people put out more than their share of effort in relationships that are not ideally balanced in regard to effort.

When talking with your grandchild about why certain people are attractive, look at the behaviors of those people. Children need to discover that Jonny Depp and Angelina Jolie are attractive in their films for a combination of reasons. Their physical characteristics are not easily copied, but look carefully at how Jonny Depp plays his romantic scenes. He's concerned, involved, and ready to be a part of his leading lady's solution to problems.

Isn't this the fantasy, *"If he were here, he would be interested in me, too?"* When a film wishes to portray the disillusionment of the common fellow who pursues a beautiful and too-sophisticated woman, the script doesn't turn her ugly—just vain, uninterested and not capable of liking others.

4. The Media Can Help Communication About Social Skills.

Grandparents can use the popularity of the media with teenagers to trigger listening times. When child-teens and grandparents watch a TV show together or read the same magazine article, they can talk it over. Ask your fellow viewers about the situations or characters' actions. Raise questions and then listen, instead of moralizing. Listening helps children express their developing views; telling them what to think turns them off to the adult and the topic.

When Grandma and Grampa make separate lists of topics they discuss with their grandchild-teen, TV programs often show up on the list. Parents may see TV as an intruder to parental influence, but it is also a rich source of neutral, lively subjects for conversation, especially when adults and children watch together.

Grampa: *"What did you think of that show?"*

Lisa: *"The babies were the best part of the show! They were cute."*

Grampa: *"Never cried or needed diaper*

changes."

Lisa: *"Not very realistic, I guess, but I liked the way the grampa talked to the twins."*

Grampa: *"Babies need to hear a lot of talk to learn."*

TV situations are not threatening because they happen to someone else, and your grandchild has as much information as you do since both of you watched the same show. Help your grandchildren react to and question TV shows, instead of simply letting them be passive viewers. You have your attitudes and answers to life's questions, and TV can help the kids form their views, especially when someone is there to listen and ask questions.

How the media portray sexuality is a good example. TV and magazines sell products by using material about sex to attract and keep their audience. They show sex in favorable ways, while omitting negatives. Casual and irresponsible sex seems like innocent fun with no consequences on TV, but we are not shown the realistic side with stress and need for understanding and intimacy on many levels. We are often spared any discussion of unwanted pregnancy, abortion, and the nine-month stresses of pregnancy without a husband's support—much less the anxiety of expectations and commitment. Television rarely shows the caring for a sick baby.

In a short time span the media can't possibly cover the 18 or more years it takes to raise a person from baby to adult or the lifetime commitment of becoming a parent. Grandparents who discuss media's omissions with their grandchildren can raise questions about these issues occasionally and provide a means to help children-teens develop their own adjustment to sexuality.

5. Talking About Sex.

If sexual *behavior* doesn't seem to qualify for your list of priority concerns about your very young grandson or daughter, his or her *preoccupation* with the topic should earn it a place on the list. The body of a pre-teen may still be undergoing sexual development, but the mind is far ahead.

Total ignorance of sexual matters is not possible today because of peers and the media. Sex education at school can provide the objective facts, but your child's anxieties and confusions are not likely to be trotted out for all to hear at school.

Of course, sex is an emotional issue, so even a grandparent needs to examine his/her own feelings before talking with the grandkids. Which topics are you ready to deal with? Dating? Differences between sex drives of girls and boys? Sex before marriage? Building a serious relationship? Contraception? Pregnancy? Disease? Decide what you think is important for your grandchildren to understand first; then prepare to be a listener your child-teenager can count on.

One grandmother told me about a conversation with her granddaughter that seemed to start with her curiosity about how Grandma and her husband decided to have children. But as you will see, Marie was really looking for information about her own risks. It went like this:

Marie: *"Grandma, you and Grampa had Mom right after you were married?"*

Grandma: *"No, Marie, it was a few years."*

Marie: *"Why did you wait?"*

Grandma: *"We worked for a couple of years, and then when we wanted children, we just...didn't."*

Marie: *"So it took a long time?"*

Grandma: *"Yes, sometimes it does."*

Marie: *"So you didn't have a baby right off, right?"*

Grandma: *"No, not right off."*

Marie: *"Lauren said you could have a baby after... just one time—she's always spouting off."*

Grandma: *"It could happen right off."*

Marie: *"But it wouldn't, if you are careful."*

Grandma had a choice at this point. She could have said, *"Marie, I know what you're thinking and let me tell you you'd better stop thinking about anything like that! You could get pregnant easily, get a disease, and anyway it's wrong to go around thinking about getting into a relationship like that at your age."* But Grandma avoided the correction and warnings and she kept the conversation away from a confrontation. So it went like this:

Grandma: *"It's hard to be careful in that situation."*

Marie: *"But if you use the right thing..."*

Grandma: *"What's the right thing?"*

Marie: *"Well, you know, a condom."*

Grandma: *"Still a chance of getting pregnant."*

Marie: *"Well, how about something else? The pill."*

Grandma: *"That works pretty well, but it doesn't protect you from diseases."*

Marie: *"Both then. Why not both?"*

Grandma: *"Both is good. Staying on the pill too*

long is not good."

Marie: *"You could use timing."*

Grandma: *"Not very reliable."*

Marie: *"This is too complicated."*

Grandma: *"Well, in a long-term relationship you can talk this all out, and it's not so embarrassing, but in dating, the practical part is too embarrassing to talk about, and that's where the trouble starts."*

Marie: *"I guess."*

You may still be worried about Marie. The talk doesn't end with much assurance about what she's going to do next. But the talk never had a chance of guaranteeing Marie's future; the best Grandma could hope for is to provide more guidance to keep Marie on the right path. This is not a place for an efficiency-oriented demand or proclamation and, a talk, too short on facts, will only lead Marie to ask someone else.

One mother told me, *"I don't have time for all that dancing around. I just tell them."* I would advise making time for dancing around—take time away from something less important. Otherwise, you'll never learn what it was they wanted you to tell them.

"Grandma, I think I have a problem." We all

hope this problem turns out to be simple and not too serious—maybe a tough homework assignment or a fellow student with bad social skills. We hope it is not the forever life-changing announcement. But you might have a moment of fear if you have heard the statistics concerning teenage pregnancies.

How should a grandparent talk to his or her child-teen about this sensitive subject? Avoiding the topic and withholding information will not postpone the risks. "If I don't know how to do it safely, I won't do it," is not a popular childhood motto.

A conversation too short, too fast, or with too many family members chiming in, is not likely to help.

Make sure your grandchild or teenager gets the facts straight. One teenage girl told me, "I want to be safe. If I have sex, I always sneak one of Mom's pills the next day."

In the United States, teenage daughters have a 1 in 20 chance of becoming pregnant, and both sons and daughters are at three times that risk for sexually transmitted diseases.

This is not just a "girl problem."

Before you talk with your grandchild, a little self-inspection is in order. What do you want to say about your grandson's responsibilities in a relationship? What message does he get in the non-serious moments about his (and his Grampa's) attitude toward women and sex? What do you want to say about contraceptives? Abortion? At what age do you want to talk about these topics?

The fathers who cause high school teenage pregnancies are usually long out of high school themselves, so your granddaughter needs to be cautioned about these "older kids" and your 17-and-something grandson may need some cautions about this temptation.

Alcohol is the most common excuse young women give for making the big mistake. What attitudes should we model on this subject?

When it's time to get serious, remember all those listening skills. Keep your pace of conversation slow. Reserve your answers and advice until your "grand-teenager" has a chance to express his/her opinion. Before you give all your guidance, you need to learn what they know, or think they know.

Remember that one session on this topic will not be enough, so conclusions that begin with "You should...," "Don't ever...," and "Be careful not to..." don't have to be said in the first conversation.

Take your time on this subject, it may be the most important part of your influence on your grandson's or daughter's future.

6. Set Priorities, Raise Questions and Listen.

Grandparents report success from initial talks with their grandchildren when they have opened communication lines. The important part, and the hardest part, for your grandchildren, is listening. For example, we grandparents want to make our cases for postponing sex, but your grandchildren can probably only tolerate one point before feeling frustrated at being the listener.

With Granddaughters. Grandma brought up building ideal relationships with Caitlin while they were walking around the lake. Grandma had thought about it and had written down her ideas. She knew she wouldn't be able to say everything, but she had her ideas in mind: building a relationship of knowledge and trust with someone of the opposite sex takes a lot of time, time to learn the other person's interests, values, goals, and dreams. Trust and commitment increase slowly from small bits of time spent together. The eventual bond of marriage is built on many times of trust and caring.

Grandma: *"What do you want from an ideal relationship with a boy?"*

Caitlin: *"I don't know. Gee, I guess respect for me and my ideas. Someone who is there*

for me, someone who likes sports, and has a sense of humor."

Grandma: *"I think respect is important too. And trust. I learned to trust your Grampa when I saw him every day and we talked, over snacks, between classes."*

Caitlin: *"You and Grampa knew each other less than a year before you were married."*

Grandma: *"Yes, but we spent time together every day talking about our pasts, present, and futures. We came to know the real persons under our college student shells."*

Caitlin: *"I'll never find a man like Grampa. The guys I know don't begin to have it together."*

Grandma: *"Men take time to grow up."*

Caitlin: *"They have a long way to go!"*

And Caitlin does, too. But she has Grandma and Grampa to listen and share her journey.

Grampa should plan his listening session with Caitlin, too. He wants her to understand that when boys have sex, they don't always feel commitment, whereas girls often think having sex *means* commitment. Also, he wants her to realize that contraception before marriage is more likely to be used incorrectly, but teens don't like to hear that, because it implies they're not smart. So instead of trying to get across his whole agenda, Grampa will try to do something much harder, be a neutral, encouraging listener most of the time.

Grampa: *"In your family life class, did they discuss differences in the sex drive between girls and guys?"*

Caitlin: *"Gosh, we heard more about physical differences than drives. But our teacher said boys have stronger feelings about sex than girls. Do you think that's right?"*

Grampa: *"Well, different anyway. Boys have sex on their minds a lot of the time!"*

Caitlin: *"Yeah, the boys make so much of it when someone says something even a little bit sexy in class."*

Grampa: *"Guys can be more inconsiderate and selfish than girls about sex. It's good to know that."*

If Caitlin continues to find a reliable listener in Grampa, he may be able to help her understand her own sexual adjustment and the opposite sex.

With Grandsons. Grandparents need to keep the lines open with grandsons as well as daughters. Boys appreciate Grampas and Grandmas taking time to listen and talk about questions to help their grandson's sexual adjustments too.

Before Todd had his first serious date alone, he and Grampa spent a weekend camping together. Grampa noted the important things he wanted Todd to know:

- If you postpone sex you get to know the other person without the stress, preoccupation and anxiety of sex with no real relationship.
- Waiting means you can both trust each other about sex, and you don't have to hide what you're doing from friends or parents.
- If you wait for sex, you have a better chance avoiding an unwanted pregnancy, abortion, or disease.

The sex drive is a very strong want, but it's a short-term need; building a relationship of trust and caring is both a short and long-term need.

Grampa: *"What does a girl want in going out?"*

Todd: *"A good time, I guess, and a lot of talking."*

Grampa: *"Just to get to know you."*

Todd: *"I guess."*

Grampa: *"You talk a lot on dates?"*

Todd: *"Yeah."*

Grampa: *"Do you ask a lot about her?"*

Todd: *"Sometimes. Not much, I guess."*

Grampa: *"People like someone who asks them about themselves—just as you like it."*

Grampa's on his way to helping Todd learn about relationships by asking questions and letting Todd explore his problem. Todd may even discover that his need is not as simple as just sex, but includes companionship and intimacy at many levels.

Questions and stories help keep communication flowing.

Grampa: *"How was your date?"*

Todd: *"OK, but Jennifer and I just don't get along so well anymore."*

Grampa: *"You're having some rough spots now."*

Todd: *"Yeah, she likes those horror movies. We always seem to do her thing."*

Grampa: *"What did she think of your new shirt?"*

Todd: *"OK, I guess. She didn't say. Sounds like she doesn't care, doesn't it?"*

Grampa: *"A little."* Grampa's listening helped, and when Todd is ready, he'll find someone who cares more.

Grandma: *"How was the movie last night, Susan?"*

Susan: *"Pretty good. Coming out we started talking to Jim and his friends."*

Grandma: *"He's a senior, right?"*

Susan: *"Yeah, and he comes on strong. They gave us a ride back, and he was all over me! He's nice, though. I wish he'd ask me out, but he won't unless I, you know, do more."*

Grandma: *"I had a boyfriend like that once."*

Susan: *"What did you do?"*

Grandma: *"Well, not much. I told him where I stood, and we got along, but it was always a running battle. He'd try something, and I'd always put him off. It didn't last long."*

Susan: *"He stopped asking you out?"*

Grandma: *"Yes, we were both tired of the struggle. I dated someone else, and 'Come-On-Strong' looked for someone more... willing."*

Finding out that Grandma went through similar experiences, Susan feels more confident. Let's look at two more cases, Kendra and Derek.

Grandma: *"How was your date last night?"*

Kendra: *"Oh, fine, I guess."*

Grandma: *"Just 'fine'?"*

Kendra: *"Tom and I always end up in the same old argument."*

Grandma: *"Really? About what?"*

Kendra: *"Well, you know, like about how far to go."*

Up to this point Grandma has been pretty neutral and not argumentative. But conversations with teenagers can have a turning point if grandma signals her intention to be authoritarian. Let's have Grandma come up with a question that keeps the conversation in Kendra's control.

Grandma: *"What kinds of arguments come up?"* (Grandma interested, not angry or opinionated, yet.)

Kendra: *"Oh, he says it won't make any problems."*

Grandma: *"No problems? Just like a man! There are lots of problems. For example . . ."*

Well, Grandma has slipped into a lecture mode, and Kendra is probably moving toward the door, so let's take this one back and replace it with . . .

Grandma: *"Well, I guess you think there would be some problems."* (Again the control of the conversation goes back to Kendra.)

Kendra: *"Tom thinks there's no problem. Right,*

for him, maybe!"

Grandma: *"Right."*

Kendra: *"Yeah, it's no risk for him!"*

Grandma: *"Being pregnant, you mean."*

Kendra: *"Yes!"*

Grandma: *"Good point."*

Kendra's position seems stronger now and straighter in her mind. No need for closing arguments. Let Grandma and Kendra walk out in agreement. It's the most we could hope for and extracting a promise would not have as great an influence as Kendra's own conviction that she is right.

Talk of sex with an open channel for your "grandteen" to talk, discover, and state opinions will result in a less confused person who is more likely to make reasonable decisions.

Grandma's talk with Kendra can expand to the general topic of relationships so that the role of sex for good and bad can be understood. How has it worked out for Kendra's other friends? Let's look at a grandfather-grandson example.

Derek: *"Girls can be such a pain!"*

Grampa: *"How so?"*

Derek: *"Well, they don't know what they want.*

They want to go out, but then they get, well, standoffish."

Grampa: *"They don't want to go far enough?"*

Derek: *"Well, yeah. It's not like we're doing, you know, everything!"*

Grampa: *"You don't want to do that?"*

Derek: *"Well, I mean I don't expect it."*

Grampa: *"Until later."*

Derek: *"Yeah."*

Grampa: *"You could get in a lot of trouble with sex."*

That's too argumentative. Let's give Grampa the chance we gave Grandma. Grampa seemed to get by the choice between authoritarian and helpful at first, but now he's ready to lecture. Grampa's last remark starts with *"you,"* and it is not hard to figure what's coming. So in Grampa's second try let's give him some *"it"* rather than *"you"* statements. That should provide a little less confrontation and a little more learning.

Grampa: *"It can be a lot of trouble."*

Derek: *"Well, you have to be careful."*

Grampa: *"You're right. But I was thinking of the social trouble."*

Derek: *"I don't get it."*

Grampa: *"Well, don't people think of sex as a kind of permanent commitment?"*

Derek: *"I guess. That was the problem with Tom and Kendra. They broke up in a big argument."*

Grampa: *"I guess that's one of the problems. Sometimes sex makes a relationship much deeper for one person than the other. Especially if they barely know each other."*

Derek: *"Well, you should be sure of the relationship."*

Grampa: *"It takes time."*

Derek: *"Yeah."*

The "lot of trouble" Grampa had in mind in the first reaction can now come up by discussing other people, not Derek. For example, how has it been for Derek's friends, Tom and Kendra? How does the media handle relationships, sex roles, and "trouble"? Exploring the one-sidedness of TV can appeal to a teen's occasional negative focus. You hardly ever get a close look at a messy diaper change on TV. Realistic decisions will come from realistic views provided by long, open conversations.

7. A Disposition Creates Its Own Surroundings.

When kids imitate bad dispositions, they must

use threats in a subtle way because they are less powerful than adults. Fighting back, a child-teen puts off her parents or teacher and may put off their requests for work. That reaction creates further negative reactions from adults who are then viewed by many teenagers as people with predictable cynical expectations of kids.

Consider Lisa at age 14. She has developed a negative attitude and is often cynical and pessimistic at school. You can imagine that it is easy to feel uncomfortable or aggravated around her. At home with her family, Lisa receives a bit more attention, but the aggravation and frustration that others feel usually shows through:

Grandma: *"How was school today, Lisa?"*
Lisa: *"OK."*
Grandma: *"Well, tell me about it!"*
Lisa: *"Do you have to know everything?"*
Grandma: *"I was just interested."*
Lisa: *"Just leave me alone."*

Lisa is a non-rewarder. She's self-centered, thinking little of others and asking little of them. She's no trouble, but somehow she's still troublesome. She brings out the worst in others, and then reacts to that by getting worse herself. The cycle continues. To break the cycle, someone will have to be big enough to not play the game. That requires love, because it means performing good social behavior with no support from Lisa, possibly with punishment from her instead.

Lisa herself might grow up enough to be the "someone" who will break the cycle someday. However, in the short run, it's not likely that anyone will spontaneously change. The most likely adjustment Lisa will make is to *"give them back what they give me."* If they give you bad behavior, let them taste their own medicine! Punishment for punishment; silence for silence, or even, silence for punishment *("They won't get anything out of me!")*.

Lisa may extend her use of punishment and later, learn to use warnings of punishments to coerce her teacher or parent. If demands are not met, she increases the intensity of the demand, and then she uses nastiness or possibly a tantrum. It's coercion.

Adults may learn to avoid all this punishment by giving in early. Giving in serves as reward to Lisa, but it also rewards the adults because they successfully avoid Lisa's escalating nastiness. It is a common parent-child relationship where *the child's bad behavior is rewarded* by getting undeserved privileges or avoiding work, and a parent's "giving in" is rewarded by successfully avoiding the threat of more bad behavior. It's a case of negative reinforcement for parents and positive reinforcement for Lisa.

In order to have an effect on Lisa, the adults around her will need to model and maintain a more positive disposition than Lisa does.

8. Children, Parents and Grandparents Learn Each Other's Habits.

A grandson or daughter's most common reaction to everyday problems will probably be to imitate people he or she lives with at home and in school. Children becoming teens imitate *styles* of adults more often than specific adult behaviors.

Attitudes toward others, conversational style and temperament are the durable characteristics of adults that the kids copy. The result is a general disposition made up of habits and styles of encouragement and punishment from others. A child can easily acquire a disposition almost entirely from the family air!

The disposition to punish and correct others can be learned just as easily as the disposition to encourage others. But to learn to police your disposition is a difficult task. There are no planned consequences for *you* as an adult. Adults change by practice with encouragements just as children do.

The positive approach emphasizes reward—not necessarily material ones, but approval, praise, smiling, etc. The job becomes more pleasant for you as a grandparent and leaves you with a child who is still informative, friendly, responsive, and not always wanting to go somewhere else!

A positive reaction is much more efficient because it says that out of all the things he could have done, this is one of the right ones. A rewarding reaction is more difficult, however, because it takes time to decide what you want to reward and how to do it. We're more likely to already know what we want to punish, and how we would do it.

Suggestion 7: The Bad Habits of Alcohol, Drugs, and Cars

"I figure, you know, what do I have to lose?"

When the dangerous subjects come up, what's the best way to handle it? No one can tell you exactly what to say, but first, Grandma and Grampa might do some intense soul-searching of their own attitudes. Some facts presented here may help with your preparation.

1. Is Alcohol the Most Dangerous Substance?
Statistics tell us that your grandchildren are more likely to abuse alcohol than any of those other dangerous substances. Drugs often produce the most dramatic problems, but in terms of number of abusers, alcohol still wins. Drug symptoms will be discussed in the next section, but the first attention goes to alcohol because it's more available, and its interaction with other substances can be so lethal.

Alcohol abusers are defined as persons whose

drinking habits produce excessive absenteeism from work or school and complaints from friends and family. By this definition one-quarter of our teens are classified as alcohol abusers by the time they reach college age. Your grandchild is picking up messages everyday about alcohol use and abuse.

In earlier generations the risks of alcohol and drugs were most frequently restricted to older teenagers. Yet in these tough times, stories of sad behaviors and sad consequences reach down to eight-year-olds. The accident and death rates are now greater in earlier generations.

2. Don't Send the Wrong Messages.

The way you listen and teach, and the role model you present, all influence risks in the dangerous business of growing up. The smothering wave of media hype and information will present all the possibilities of the abusive behaviors. Your listening can help straighten out the information; your observations and your model can highlight the successes in following the right direction.

"Grampa, do you drink?"

"I've had a beer on a hot day and wine sometimes."

"How does it make you feel?"

"I don't drink enough to feel anything. I've learned it just makes me sleepy right away and sick later. Why do you ask?"

"I was just wondering. John's father was drinking a beer the other day."

"It's not a good habit, and it's been shown to be hard on young brains."

"Can I try it?"

"Maybe when you are older."

I think most of us grandparents would feel uncomfortable in this conversation. We are in the dangerous area of hypocrisy, and not much progress is being made. As far as extracting a guarantee of abstinence from a child, we may feel impatient with this Grampa. But in building an attitude, a little progress on the big job may have been accomplished.

The topic is so dangerous that the necessary long talks themselves seem dangerous. When our own shortcomings are dragged out for review, our temptation is to fall back on lecturing. The lecture will be an attempt to extract a promise of abstinence from our grandson or daughter, but the only guarantee of safe behavior is in the long term of establishing values. I would give this Grampa high marks for keeping his eye on that goal.

Listening is critical in the discussions of dangerous behaviors. A feeling of confidence and self-esteem, as overworked as those terms are in child-rearing, are the best protection we have to offer children today.

Don't send the message that alcohol is a problem solver. Your model is one of the best predictors of later drinking habits. Yet families that approve of moderate alcohol use, for example, Jewish families where wine is a part of religious services, do not show a greater risk of teenage alcohol abuse. The important factor seems to be the message concerning the role of alcohol consumption. *"I've had a tough day; I need a drink!"* is a message that alcohol can solve lots of problems. This is not a good message for young ears.

Don't send the message that alcohol is necessary for social situations. The idea that stress or social inhibitions are eased by alcohol is part of the foundation of alcohol dependence. Using alcohol for its temporary relaxing effect only postpones learning better social skills. The habit also becomes entrenched long before the person becomes addicted in other ways. So, for example, many people not yet addicted can't enjoy a party until alcohol has had its effect.

TV and other media glamorize alcohol and imply that alcohol is essential to having a good time. *"Things go better with Bud"* is not necessarily true, as many of us adults have learned.

Don't send the message that behavior under the influence of alcohol is more honest, natural, or free. Children often think less thoughtful behavior is more genuine. The message that behavior under the influence is less filtered by inhibitions and thoughtfulness, shouldn't lead to the conclusion these actions are better. Inhibitions are learned from experience, and thoughtfulness is a precious human quality.

Grandparents need to set a healthy model of problem-solving based on skills and experience. When teens depend on alcohol to break down social inhibitions, the breakdown of sexual inhibitions will quickly become the next bad habit. Intoxication is the most common reason given for unsafe sex in surveys of teenagers.

Spending time with your grandchildren sends the message that they are valuable. A child who feels valued and capable is less likely to start using alcohol than children who feel they have *"nothing to lose."* Recognize your teen as an increasingly capable, valued family member.

3. Drugs and Self-Esteem.

I'm not going to have a drink for lunch today, nor drugs this afternoon. The statistics would say you will probably avoid the same things. Why? Because we both feel we have too much to lose. We have family and work responsibilities, and goals we have set for ourselves. We hope to make a contribution to our community and family and have some success in our jobs. Too much to lose—that's how we see ourselves.

Who will point out what wonderful talents and potentials a teen has to lose? My conversation with a drug-experimenting pre-teen is tragically typical:

"So let me get this straight. You took some white powder your friend had in his garage, put it on a piece of glass in a little row. Then you took a straw and sucked it up your nose?"

"Well, yeah."

"What about the dirt, let alone the stuff itself. How could you be sure it was clean or even made of what your friend said it was?"

"Well, I didn't know, but I figure, you know, what do I have to lose?"

(My parent outrage almost pops out.) *"What do you have to lose!? You've got your whole life ahead of you ..."*

I know what I have to lose, why doesn't this kid know what *he* has to lose? All those lectures in school—about health, brain damage, infection, addiction, and the violence of the people involved in these trades—and he still can ask, "What do I have to lose?"

The lectures are to groups, of course, and they leave out the personal abilities, individual prospects and talents of the individuals. Who will tell our grandsons and daughters what they, personally, have to lose?

How does a teen learn to value himself, learn what he has to lose? That self-respect will come from developing competencies—even everyday ones like cooking, keeping track of money, and doing domestic chores. One of the best protections against dangerous behaviors is the family habit of providing satisfying tasks that build confidence.

One 12-year-old boy said to me that he told his friends he couldn't cruise the mall that day because,

"I make dinner on Tuesdays, and I already bought the stuff." There's a small step in the direction of self-confidence.

4. Medications: "I didn't get my pill today, can I help it?"

What's the answer to those annoying outbursts from the kids—the crying fits and the hyperactivity? Even when medications are necessary, both parents and physicians are worried about long-term effects and hope to add natural long-term remedies that will provide a more fundamental adjustment.

Adults may view the problem as a product of unfortunate circumstances. For example, a parent will say, "He has a hard time behaving because he was upset when his father and I divorced." Or, "He was upset when I remarried." Other parents suspect that bipolar symptoms exist in one or both sides of the family tree.

Of course, any of these speculations could be true, or partly true, but regardless of underlying causes, changing a child-teen's behavior using careful reactions may hold the only hope for long-term improvement.

Studies by the U.S. Department of Agriculture

show children and teens guzzle 64 gallons of soft drinks a year with an average of 38 milligrams of caffeine in every ounce. For adults, it's coffee and, if it's fancy coffee, the caffeine may be over 200 milligrams per cup.

After the temporary boost in energy, there's the inevitable drop in energy and disposition that follows. A re-supply of caffeine will produce another burst of energy, but an addiction is beginning to form just to avoid the downturn-aftereffect. Addiction is fundamentally a negative reinforcement effect (see part 2 of Suggestion 4).

Hofstra University Professor Jennifer Schare studied 400 preschoolers for a year and found that the heavy users of caffeine had more "uncontrollable energy," which could be, and occasionally was, diagnosed as ADHD. If caffeine is occasional, provided at school but not at home, for example, a "bipolar disorder" might be suspected. At school he is wired and always in trouble, but at home he calms down but is grumpy. Caffeine effects and the additional sleep disturbance that comes with them provide pharmaceutical companies with a host of prescriptions for "disturbed" children.

Physicians often recommend less than 100

milligrams of caffeine per day—two ounces of most colas—for the whole day. Why they recommend any at all is hard to understand.

In addition to a diet that contains caffeine and sugar in large quantities, food allergies can add to the problem. The National Institutes of Health reports that 50 million Americans suffer from allergic diseases, and 54 percent test positive for one or more allergens. The most common disruptive culprits in children's diet besides caffeine and sugar are eggs, milk products, citrus fruits, nuts, tomatoes, bananas and certain food additives.

In the United States, processed foods contain nearly 7,000 new additives all approved for use in our food since the 1940s. Most were not heard of a century ago. By contrast, Northern Europeans have approved only about 70 of the 7,000 food additives that are legal over here. That may explain some of our expanding allergies.

"Food intolerances" occur when the digestive process rejects a certain kind of food. Other problems are food allergies in which certain (usually stomach) tissues are irritated by the food. In either case, keeping careful records of what your grandchild or teenager eats and when he acts up can identify foods that produce behavioral side effects.

A teenager who is sensitive to particular foods is likely to be more frequently irritated by parents, teachers and siblings. He or she is not likely to understand that disrupted sleep and the resulting unhappiness may be an additional allergy symptom along with his/her runny nose, stuffiness, wheezing, stomach ache, itchy eyes or muscle ache. Even his or her parents may not recognize the connection.

We should be cautious in focusing on one solution for a troublesome child. Here's a true example.

When Jeff was six, he was a model child. He was easy-going and seldom any trouble at school, but when he started second grade, he became agitated and impatient and fought with other students. Tantrums became a daily burden at home and in school. At home the tantrums usually built up around bedtime or later at night when he woke up restless and irritated.

Had he been assigned to a bad teacher? Did something happen at home?

I knew Jeff's mother well. She was a steady, dedicated and loving Mom. Because of the surprising change in Jeff's character, I asked her to keep a record of everything Jeff ate and when disruptions happened. Although Jeff was already on some medication for his disruptive behavior, Mom took it as a challenge to note every scrap and snack that he had. In six weeks her records showed a peculiar but common event: Every time Jeff had pizza, his behavior got worse.

So we started the pizza experiment. No pizza for two weeks and the frequency of his tantrums went down a little, but his troubles at school and home continued.

There was no dramatic result until Jeff's Mom (remember, she's the dedicated type) declared all tomato products off limits for the family. That's not an easy task when you think about all the sources – ketchup, salads, pizzas, salad dressings, spaghetti sauce, casseroles and the list goes on. But it turned out Jeff had an allergy.

Without tomatoes, Jeff's old self started coming back, but every time he slipped up (one time we discovered tomato was in the salad dressing), the irritations returned. To protect Jeff (and everyone else), the whole family went off tomatoes.

Where do such allergies come from? It's a mystery how we get these sensitivities, but our expanding diet in the U.S. certainly helps us find them. Oranges from Florida are not just a holiday treat any more, and milk no longer comes from a farm in your county. You can't even be sure your food comes from this hemisphere. The greater the variety of food sources you sample, the more likely you are to take in something that disagrees with you.

Jeff, by the way, grew up to be an emergency room physician. He is still his easy-going self, and he's still off tomatoes.

Certainly diet, allergies, parental and grandparental habits play a role in these problems. Even if medications are already a part of the answer, a record of bad behavior as well as allergic reactions, variations in parental habits and diet may show other sources of the problem.

Nevertheless, 350 million doses of Ritalin, Adderall, and Dexedrine will be given this year in the U.S. to control bad behavior in children—triple the doses given in all other countries put together. In many cases these medications are helpful, but allergy testing and careful recording of everything a child-teen eats and the time he eats it can show aggravating sensitivities that cause family problems.

Even a teenager correctly diagnosed with Autism

or attention deficit/hyperactivity disorder (ADHD) is not merely afflicted with one wrong process. Diet and what happens next can still influence bad habits. The thoughtful use of reactions and consequences, watching for good behaviors to highlight and encouraging self-esteem through useful tasks, all of these remain a part of the answer to bad social habits.

Prescriptions can be a convenient answer to common rowdiness, sleeplessness and school problems, but medications can cover up other causes.

Since behaviors are partly controlled by what happens before and after, I also ask parents to include a record of the events just before and after the problem behavior surfaces. Two hours of TV right before the melt-down or an entertaining argument with Grandma can indicate an answer that would help as much as any pill.

The solution will also have to include what is good about our problem-child's behavior. What do we want to encourage, and how can we encourage it? If he does his homework, then what happens? Do we look it over and admire the work or go on to getting dinner ready because, for the moment, the problem is solved?

Medications can be life-savers for parents

suffering with a severely disturbed child. Drug companies have a right to be proud of the help they provide. But it is not right to belittle environmental effects just because medications can reduce the symptoms.

Nearly all grandparents have been amazed by a healthy child finding 200 ways to sit on a chair, 10 ways to lose his hat, and 30 ways to tangle shoelaces. Activity, even hyperactivity, seems to be just part of growing up.

But one child in ten suffers from behavioral disorders such as ADHD, separation anxiety, or social phobia. And about 3.4 million U.S. children under 18 are said to be seriously depressed. Ritalin and similar medications are life-savers and family-savers for those situations in which a child or teenager is extremely agitated for long periods every day.

5. Drugs and Other Troubles after School.

The prime time for juvenile crime is from 2 to 6 p.m. You might think it would be at night, but for this young age group, a survey found violent juvenile crime peaked between 3 and 4 p.m. "Fight Crime: Invest in Kids of California," a nonprofit organization, conducted the survey of their state's law enforcement agencies in 1999.

Even in the rest of the nation, after-school hours are the most dangerous hours for serious car accidents involving teenagers. Vandalism, theft and violent crimes are reduced when kids attend after-school programs. Without continued support from parents and schools for a variety of after-school programs, troubles multiply.

After-school programs are not the whole answer to the drug problem, but an understanding of the many circumstances that sometimes influence drug-taking can help.

We were all shocked in the 60's and 70's to find drugs becoming common in affluent schools. We should have known that these would be the most obvious targets. Addicts need money, lots of money, and they hope to get it from our kids. A pusher isn't interested in a kid who doesn't have much money. Your grandchildren should not carry any more money than necessary to school or afternoon outings.

Try to stay informed about the money your grandchild-teen has. How much does she make from her job? Where does her money go? Better spent on clothes and fun than available for trouble.

Maybe taking a child for an outing would be a better birthday present than cash or a check.

Changes in your grandchild's appetite, hours of sleep, and symptoms that seem like an allergy or cold but linger too long, should be explored.

Some of us want to show our grandchildren that Grandma and Grampa are "cool" about drugs. When we approve of our own drug use or misuse of medications and alcohol, it encourages an irresponsible attitude in our kids and sets the stage for trouble.

Remember, however, that talk about drugs and other adventurous and dangerous activities are favorite topics for all healthy kids. They need this free conversation as a way of exploring these topics easily. Parents and grandparents around the children should not react too impulsively to just talk and save dramatic reactions for a time when the concrete evidence of drug or alcohol use is in.

As a treatment for ADHD, Ritalin increases nervous system alertness and thereby increases focus and ability to concentrate. Millions of prescriptions for Ritalin are written each year to treat ADHD. The use of Adderall and Dexedrine is not far behind Ritalin in the totals for ADHD treatment, up 2,000 percent in the last two decades.

Yet a study by Drs. Adrian Angold and Jane Costello found that the majority of children and adolescents who receive these medications do not fully meet the criteria for ADHD—even with the expanded criteria for ADHD approved by the American Psychiatric Association.

Many families have made medications their first solution to behavior problems. Dr. Lawrence H. Diller, pediatrician and author of *Running on Ritalin: A Physician Reflects on Children, Society and Performance in a Pill,* concludes: *"How we deal with our kids' problems reflects our thinking and a much larger problem in our culture."* An editorial in the *Journal of the American Medical Association* reported that behavioral medications have tripled for children under five, increased 170 percent for five- to 14-year-olds and again up 300 percent for the 15- to 19-year-olds.

Many of us want a solution that requires no more work or attention beyond making sure the troublesome youngster gets his medication. Physicians also hope prescriptions will do the job. The business world hopes to sell caffeine, sugar and additives, regardless of the behavioral effects.

Limiting these in your grandchild's diet may be more effective than medications that have no proven track record with very young persons. For ADHD children who are temporarily so hot-wired they cannot be reached and cannot be taught, Ritalin can be a godsend. And a day in school can go much better for a student who would otherwise wreck a school day for himself and other students as well.

When absolutely necessary parental time is added, a grandchild-teenager in need of medication may develop and adjust to life and soon leave the medications behind. However, you will have to defend a distinction between "drugs" and medications in family discussions later on.

The concern about alcohol and drugs also requires strategies focusing on learning what is going on. The effects of experimental drug-taking, for example, may show the same symptoms parents see everyday, cold-like symptoms, changes in sleeping and eating patterns, new friends, new attitudes, new demands about money, longer hours at the mall, and hanging out. All are very normal unless they all happen at once.

It's the clustering that should ring an alarm. When the hangout, the mall or corner, suddenly takes much more time, the sniffles become an annoyance to the whole family, demands for new curfew hours increase, and money is suddenly missing or suddenly acquired and cannot be explained, it's time to be suspicious.

"Tune in" to your grandchild's life, habits, and problems. Notice general changes in eating, sleeping, health, and friends. If you don't see your grandchildren very often, you may see changes beyond the normal growth and development that should be mentioned to your grandchild's parents.

6. Checklists for Habits and Behavior.
   Checklist No. 1: Changes in Habits
   1. Does your grandchild or teenager need more money than usual or is money missing from the house?
   2. Is he or she spending more time in his/her room with the door closed or locked?
   3. Have sleeping or eating habits changed or has irritability increased?
   4. Has he changed friends or become secretive about friends?

One Grandma told me she liked to eat dinner slowly, so she and her grandson could talk. It allowed her to learn about his activities with school and friends. When she saw an unexplained change in his appetite, she asked him about it and found out that he had started stopping off with friends at a fast food restaurant after school. She was put at ease about a possible danger sign.

Watch the Money. The drug business is about money. Where can an unemployed addict get $90 or more a day to support his habit? Recruiting new users is one of the best sources for money. Drug pushers look for kids, buyers with extra money, so your children should carry only the needed amount to school or stores. Listen for information about the money your grandson or daughter has. Encourage putting money away in savings and give thoughtful consideration to your monetary gifts. A bank account for a child-teen may seem unrelated to the drug problem, but it is, since a kid with extra pocket-money is a tempting target for a frantic user.

As much as you may think the kids will never abuse alcohol or take drugs, you need to know the signs of use. Checklist Number Two describes characteristics that all children have at one time or another. Abrupt changes in these characteristics should, however, increase your curiosity, and if you're not satisfied, you should be suspicious. This is especially true when these changes occur along with the habits listed in Checklist No. 1.

Checklist No. 2: Changes in Physical Symptoms
1. Lack of concentration; extreme agitation
2. Red eyes, watery eyes, droopy eyelids
3. Runny nose, increased infections and colds
4. Change in sleeping habits—sleeping all day, up all night
5. Slurred or garbled speech, forgetting thoughts or ideas
6. Changes in appetite, either increased or decreased; cravings for certain foods
7. Change in activity level; fatigue or hyperactivity
8. Change in appearance, becoming sloppy
9. Lack of coordination, clumsiness, stumbling, sluggishness
10. Shortness of breath, coughing, peculiar odor to breath and clothes

All children show some variety of these characteristics from time to time, so these characteristics do not necessarily indicate drug abuse. The difference that deserves attention is a cluster of abrupt changes.

"John started going with those older kids last summer, and suddenly he didn't care how he looked; he was sloppy, always sniffing, getting up later and later, and he even lost interest in soccer!"

This mother found drug paraphernalia in her son's room the first time she looked! The *cluster* of changes in social habits, attitude, and self-care were enough for her to investigate.

7. Depression.

The behavior disorder of clinical depression occurs in 4 percent of preschoolers and in about 15 to 20 percent of teenagers. The numbers for children can be higher than 20 percent because we often brush off their complaints saying they "always talk like that."

The statistics vary partly because the definition of depression varies. Preschoolers don't know the word and, with teenagers, the perception of the word depends on when you talk to them and what they say.

Yet 19 million people in the U.S. complain of depression enough to make it into the clinical medical records. In 2005, 118 million prescriptions for antidepressants were written, twice as many as in 1995, says the Center for Disease Control.

Preschoolers are the fastest growing market for antidepressants. Yet the *British Journal of Medicine* reported no scientific evidence that antidepressants work for these young children. For children under 18, Britain has banned all but Prozac which is used for complicated emotional problems.

Of course, we all get the "blues" and "feel down in the dumps" from time to time. The solution is usually an increase in physical activity—sports or exercise class—or just a change of scene.

For many of us, and especially for teenagers, diet can be a part of the problem. An 11-year-old boy half the weight of his Grampa can get far too much sugar from a candy bar or an overdose of fat or caffeine from a portion that would have no effect on his Grampa.

Mental habits can also influence clinical depression. While adults can take encouragement from looking ahead to summer activities or vacations, teenagers are shortsighted. If homework is due tomorrow morning, depression can develop because the prospect of friends coming over tomorrow afternoon is too far in the future as is any upcoming weekend fun.

A child-teen's active imagination concerning the magical powers of Harry Potter or the dreams of becoming a soccer star may serve an important antidepressant purpose for a person who has not yet developed the necessary foresight to form realistic goals beyond next week.

In cases where dreams of future success are not enough to pull a grumpy teenager out of depression, a review of activities, diet, and mental habits may help grandparents understand the cause of their grandchild's depression. Common symptoms of depression are fatigue, lack of energy, and bad temper. Also, irritability, fear, tension and anxiety are common symptoms as well as a drop in school performance and repeated physical complaints without medical cause (headaches, stomach aches, aching arm or legs).

Of course all of these behaviors occur in all children and most depression is usually temporary. Excessive and continuing amounts of these symptoms deserve immediate professional advice.

Allow your grandchild-teen space and time. Keep caffeine at absolute zero. Alcohol use by children is never appropriate. Learn more about any medications your grandchild is taking. Discourage meal skipping. Regular meals, sleep, and routines are a crucial part of a child's ability to cope.

Take time to be a part of your adolescent's physical activity. It will help you as well as them, and it will be an opportunity to listen and understand. Activities such as tennis, swimming, and bicycling can last a lifetime. Team sports (soccer, football and baseball) may fade away in the adult years. Sharing hobbies such as stamp collecting, rock collecting, model building offer opportunities for easy conversations.

Communication can be just what the doctor (should have) ordered when a child needs to tell someone how scary the world sometimes seems. And companionship helps in moments when TV heroes and stars are unattainable, and a grandchild needs a friend. Love, attention and support from Grandma and Grampa will help protect a vulnerable child from the promises that "understanding predators" seem to offer. The best thing to spend on the kids is time.

8. Smoking.

I haven't seen any plans for tobacco companies to go out of business, so I guess they are counting on somebody's children to fill in for smokers who die off. During the first decades of our new century, nearly 3,000 American children under 18 began daily smoking every day. In 2014, there was evidence of a growing preference for E-cigarettes among the new teenage smokers. However, this choice still includes nicotine which may lead to addiction to regular cigarettes. If your child delays joining the ranks, there are good consequences.

For example, two teeth. Yes, smokers lose, on the average, two more teeth each decade than nonsmokers. So just delaying smoking from eight until 18 saves two teeth! Of course another 10 teeth are goners in the decades of smoking between 18 and 68.

If your grandchildren delay smoking until 20, then, in addition to saving two teeth, they are likely to delay turning prematurely gray as well, since smokers are four times more likely to turn gray prematurely. Also delaying smoking will put off balding since men who smoke are twice as likely to be bald or balding as non-smoking men.

In the long term, smokers have thinner, less elastic skin which means more wrinkles than nonsmokers. So children who wait until 25 to start smoking may look ten years younger at age 50 than classmates who started smoking at 15. I guess that's an advantage.

Starting young has other consequences. For example, young smokers have twice the likelihood of colds, flu, and respiratory disorders each year. Young smokers are also much more likely to try marijuana, and kids who have tried marijuana are twice as likely to try other drugs.

If your grandchild delays smoking until 30, other statistics kick in. First, he or she is likely to forget to start smoking at all (more than 80 percent of starters begin in high school, 90 percent before 21).

So when should your grandchild start smoking? The later the better, but never is better than later.

Actually, the percentage of young people starting to smoke hasn't changed much over the decades. But the increasing number of quitters has gone up resulting in an overall decrease in adult smokers in the U.S. from almost 80 percent in 1948 to 44 percent in 1964, to 29 percent in 1987, and 10 to 15 percent today depending on the state.

For all those ex-smokers, the health and longevity benefits start coming right away.

After 20 minutes without smoking, blood pressure decreases, pulse rate drops, body temperature of hands and feet increase.

Eight hours after quitting, carbon monoxide levels in the blood drop to normal, and the oxygen level increases to normal. After 24 hours the chance of a heart attack decreases. After two weeks circulation improves and walking is easier.

At one year, the excess risk of heart disease is decreased to half that of a smoker. Five years and stroke risk is down to that of a non-smoker. Ten years and lung cancer risk is down by half. Fifteen years and risk of heart disease and death rate are reduced to almost that of non-smokers.

Parent and grandparent smoking habits are the biggest factor in children delaying smoking or never starting at all. Over 60 percent of smokers under age 19 are children of parents who smoke (70 percent for girls and 54 percent of boys). Only 35 percent of the smokers under 19 are children of nonsmokers.

So after all the arguing about smoking statistics, what's the best thing a smoking parent or grandparent can do to steer the kids in the right direction?

Quit.

9. The Battle of the Bulge.

Obesity is an unpleasant word reserved for body fat that's out of control. For children, obesity is reached when total body weight is more than 25 percent fat for boys, 32 percent for girls. Normally, two out of ten children are in this category, but the number can reach eight out of ten children when both of their parents are obese.

In 1970 we Americans fed ourselves on 3,300 calories each day. That was the production from food companies consumed in the USA in those days. Now we are up to 3,800 calories a day according to Marion Nestlé's book, *Food Politics: How the Food Industry Influences Nutrition and Health.*

The extra 500 daily calories (equivalent to an extra banana split every day) has added 10 pounds to the average weight of a teenager compared with kids of the 90s, says the Pediatricians Research Group of Woodlands, TX. It's not surprising when you consider we tempt ourselves with over 10,000 new food products each year—mostly candy, snacks, soft drinks, baked goods, and ice creams.

Of course exercise enters in. Teenagers who report more than five hours of sedentary TV per day are five times more likely to be overweight than kids watching less than two hours each day. Snacks during TV, say, a small bag of potato chips each day, will add a half pound each week. Not much you might think, but it totals up to a 26-pound weight-gain each year.

The weight problem of our children is bulging about as fast as their parents' poundage. Back in 1991, when we were each consuming not much more than 3,300 calories per day, only Mississippi, Alabama, and West Virginia had more than 15 percent obese adults. Now more than 20 percent of adults are obese in over half the states.

No doubt the food pushers both at home and in the food business deserve some of the blame for the increases. TV with too many commercials about food and computer time with too much junk food next to the keyboard are bad routines.

Parents and grandparents can set a slow pace at family meals, even when eating out as much as Americans do. Serving sizes in restaurants are ever larger, and we should keep limits in place even there. The kids could take a doggy bag home, also.

At home, serving water at every meal and having everyone serve their plates, then putting the extra away before sitting down, are healthy habits.

Everything we do requires some effort and inconvenience. All behaviors, even getting out the donuts or hot snack, have an inconvenience. You have to get a plate, find a fork, warm it up, get a drink to go with it.

So keep the healthy food handy and ready—fruit, instead of chips, on the table, ice water instead of soft drinks in the fridge. Let the fat, salt and sugar be the ones that are the most trouble to get from the store and the most troublesome to get out at home. The kids will buy other snacks, but at least at home your diet and their diet will be better.

10. Cars and the Driving Threat.

The biggest danger to teenagers, bigger than all the other diseases and accidents of childhood put together, comes when they are almost grown. In the late teenage years, emergency room visits jump from 30 to 60 per million per day and the death rate skyrockets from one per million per day to 10!

The big change is, of course, driving.

A survey by the Liberty Mutual Insurance Company and Students Against Destructive Decisions asked high school students to interview over 1300 teenage drivers with accidents or recent near misses. All grandparents should know the survey results these dedicated students reported after interviewing their fellow drivers.

Over 68 percent of the teens who had traffic incidents said they were distracted at the crucial moment (47 percent had more than two passengers with them). Sixty-one percent were changing songs on their radio or CD player. And 36 percent said they were actually texting when the accident or near miss occurred. The same proportion said they were on their cell phone. Forty-six percent admitted they were speeding.

The number of teenage drivers involved in fatal crashes has decreased almost 55 percent since the highs in years prior to 2005. Nevertheless, 2500 lives are lost every year according to the Centers for Disease Control and Prevention. Graduated licenses that limit night driving and the restriction on the number of passengers for younger teen drivers can take much of the credit for the reduced numbers.

Parents insist on using car seats and seat belts with young children, but when the kids turn 16, all parental efforts are overwhelmed and swept aside by the shocking statistics of driving and riding with reckless friends.

Girls are now almost as much at risk as boys. In 1990, 160 of every 1000 under-18 girl-drivers wrecked their cars that year and by 2000 the number was 175. The boys are steady, but higher, at 210 per 1000 per year.

Alcohol abuse plays a large role. The National Center on Addiction and Substance Abuse reports that girls now drink just as much as boys. At the end of the 1990's, 48 percent of girls drank, and 52 percent of boys. In 2000, among high school freshmen, girls nudged out the boys for first place in reports of regular drinking—41 percent of girls and 40 percent of boys.

This summer will bring another round of deaths from drunk driving and risky driving. You don't want to wake up in the middle of the night to that terrible phone call, "This is Officer Smith of the State Police, Your teenager has been . . ."

Grandparents who hear of this call will pray, in that first heart-stopping moment, that it only involves an arrest or accident and not an injury or death.

The statistics would tell us that Mom and Dad probably gave permission for the driving plan after extracting a few promises—no deviations from the plan, no craziness, and, they might have said, no drinking—but all were likely violated at the fatal moment.

11. College is Coming, Why Some Quit and Others Stay the Course.

In my University of Maryland years as Associate Dean for Undergraduates, I gave a survey to over 500 drop-out students who came in to resign, and 500 who did not drop out. Here is what I learned.

Most students were surprised that less than 10 percent of college dropouts have failing grades. Actually, for the other 90 percent of dropouts the biggest dropout factors are housing too far away, acquired bad habits, bad health care and bad time and money management—not grades.

The top factor in dropping out is address. Living too far from campus while working long hours at an off-campus job ranks number one. If college life is limited to a job, traffic, the campus parking lot, and classes, then cutting classes (or eliminating all of them) will seem to be an easy and convenient option to reduce the hassle of their rushed life.

Bad personal habits are the next pitfall. If your grandson or daughter's usual caretakers are not around, they may feel, "Great. No more critics. I'm free to do what I want." But bad habits here have produced the poor health record of college students. You would think young students should be the healthiest part of our population but they are not.

Drinking habits have an extra danger for college women. Fifty percent of women sexually assaulted on campus were drinking at the time—making themselves more vulnerable—at least in the eyes of the one doing the assaulting. The majority of women with unwanted pregnancies in the college-age group report they were drinking at the time of the "big mistake."

Bad management makes the college dangers list because it's easy to become addicted to a job, entertainment, computers or partying as well as the more familiar habits of drugs and alcohol. Skipping meals, sleep, or exercise makes getting sick more likely. When your grandson or daughter starts feeling bad, ask about their habits and overdoses of salt, fat, sugar, and caffeine. These habits add up to poor sleeping habits and feeling tired and depressed.

College Can Be a SNAP

On the academic side, my advice to students and my own daughters boiled down to the letters in

"SNAP" which can help the study and class time pay off in grades.

The "S" in SNAP stands for Show Up. Missing class is the best predictor of a slipping grade point average. Also, nearly all students who drop out begin the downhill slide by cutting classes.

The "N" in SNAP stands for Notes. You would think the high school advice of "take notes" would be in every freshman's mind, but when they look around in their college classes they see many students who don't take notes.

Notes not only provide valuable review, they keep your attention on the class and give you extra practice if you copy them neatly later.

The "A" in SNAP stands for Active Studying. Many of my students have said, *"I can't believe I did poorly; I went through (stared at) all the pages assigned for the test!"* If reading is the assignment, get active, take reading notes. Reading notes become a source of motivation and provide bench marks so you can pick up at the right place after the phone, coffee, or pizza interruption. Never turn a page without writing down something, should be the rule.

The "P" in SNAP stands for Plan ahead. Poor time management can be a big pitfall for students on their own for the first time. Look ahead and schedule your study time. Everybody needs party time and you can't plan every minute, but a calendar will keep the priorities in order and, along with the rest of SNAP, you'll be ready for the tests.

For college freshmen, the beginning semesters produce more dropouts than all the later years of college put together. After the first semester with big class projects and final exams, the second semester looms ahead. It's a crucial time for parents and grandparents to send supportive signals to their student.

Samantha called home every week when she started college. Her grandma would respond, "Oh, Samantha, I hope you are well. We miss you so much. Your little sister is so lonely. She keeps asking, 'Is it time for Samantha's vacation yet?'"

These weekly tugs on the guilt strings were intended to let Samantha know she was loved, but she came to my office to fill out the paperwork to drop out, and she completed the job.

Samantha's college career was cut short partly because her grandma unintentionally emphasized family events that would make her homesick.

Keep the calls upbeat as much as possible, and the

pressure low about jobs, money, and grades.

Sons and daughters who juggle busy schedules of jobs and school make their family proud. But if the schedule gets too crowded with job and commuting, the college experience may be reduced to job, campus parking lot, and classes. No time left for meeting classmates, chatting with professors, or joining in the many campus activities.

Encourage your college-bound grandson or daughter to live and work close to the campus and work only the necessary hours at an outside job.

Another common reason for dropping out is loss of direction or enthusiasm for a planned major and career. Grandparents can help here also by talking over the majors represented in the early required courses and keeping the pressure to make an early decision low. One primary advantage of college is learning about the variety of life's opportunities.

Many colleges and universities have 100 or more majors, but few first-time students can name 20! No wonder over 90 percent of freshmen change their major somewhere along the way. Fifty percent will change majors more than once.

Students are often tempted to avoid this decision by leaving college for "a year off." But if college is viewed as a source of information about choices, then staying in makes sense. Little is lost by taking courses to explore the wide range of majors and careers before making this important decision. It's a long way from graduation to retirement.

An additional danger for new students comes when their mailboxes filled with offers of merchandise and credit cards. Caution your college grandchild to keep life simple with few obligations to make payments on credit, car, and clothes.

Habits concerning health (sleeping, diet, and alcohol) and management of time and money, can also be dangerous pitfalls in the college journey.

Most freshmen open a checking account and face the worries of a budget for the first time. They're on their own in budgeting their time, too. Parents and grandparents of teens with a year or two of high school left have time, now, to prepare their students for the challenges of caring for themselves.

Suggestion 8: About Social Media

Chatting with friends online is not a waste, but 800,000 sex offenders are online, too!

Notes in their personal diary may be private, but notes sent online by email, FaceBook or otherwise, should not (and usually can not) be private.

Anyone (even parents) can see any note a teen sends. Geeks with only a little computer savvy can copy and use them anywhere. You might as well spray-paint them on a fence downtown or, if they go even a little viral, then on the town water tower. Because of this possibility, an adult in the family needs to see what they type and read what comes back.

1. Computer Companions.

Teenagers average almost nine hours each day using online music or videos, TV, surfing and "chatting," the 2015 report by Common Sense Media says. The 8 to 12-year-olds average six hours a day, reports Jim Steyer, the director of the study. Over

2600 teens were interviewed.

The Kaiser Family Foundation's 2010 study said the average back then was five and a half hours for tweens, over eight hours for the 11 to 14 group and over nine for the 15 to 18-year-olds—more than the daily hours of school. The trend is definitely up.

On the positive side, schoolwork online is a growing demand for a teenager's digital attention. Yet 25 percent say their parents know little of what they watch on TV or do on social media.

Grandma: *"Jason, are you still texting on that cell phone of yours?"*

Jason: *"Yeah, I'm talking to Mark."*

Grandma: *"Mark, who?"*

Jason: *"He's my fellow fullback on the J-V soccer team."*

Grandma: *"Well. get off and come to lunch."*

Jason: *"Just a second."*

Grandma: (A minute later) *"Jason, come now!"*

Jason muttered "gotta go" while texting, then he shoved his phone in his pocket and went into the kitchen.

Grandma: *"I'm starting to think that phone was a big mistake."*

Jason: *"Grandma, Mark's a friend. We were just*

talking over the game."

Friends are an important part of life, and social media has become the connection of choice for teenagers. We need to be careful in setting limits because many teens "talk" with friends a lot more since the social media has become so popular. Grandma is right to worry about how much time is OK, but the time spent chatting with friends is not a waste.

A study by the Pew Research Center reported a lot of flirting on the net by teens, but three-quarters said they never dated someone they only met online. However, of those who had a steady friend or partner, 38 percent expected to hear from their partner every day. Eleven percent expected hourly check-ins. Forty-eight percent had resolved arguments online, and 70 percent had conversations that made them feel closer.

Among 12 to 17-year-olds in the U.S., 95 percent are online. Three out of four access the internet by cell phone or other mobile device, and 20 percent say they have received unwanted sexual solicitations.

In 2016 we had over 800,000 registered sex offenders in the United States. Of course, they are online. Seventy percent of our teens will accept "friends" regardless of whether or not they know the person making the request. Only 25 percent of 12 to 17-year-old victims told their parents of the sexual predators they met on line. Only 10 percent of victims of cyber bullying told their parents.

Girls are more likely to be harassed online with unwelcome flirting and 69 percent said that social media gives too many people a window into their private lives.

Computers and handhelds are the gadgets of choice and sometimes trouble for teens socializing with friends, surfing for informative sites, doing school work or playing games.

Socializing.

In my childhood, the family telephone was just off the living room. No school mate in my neighborhood had a phone of his own. My end of the conversation could be (and was) heard by all. If Mom answered the phone, and it was my girl friend she handed me the phone while holding up five fingers. I had five minutes to talk. Everyone listened, it cost money not to be squandered, and "time online (phone)" was a continual subject of argument.

Thankfully, the good old days are gone, and now we all have phones that can do almost anything. Yet they can also be secret, and time limits remain a problem. Children and many adults have to learn what is rude and when to turn off the gadget.

The Internet may establish a fear of missing out that keeps a teenager up to the wee hours. He might not only fear missing out, but he might also fear missing <u>anything</u>, says Sherry Turkie in her review of high-tech gadgets in the lives of teenagers. Her book is *Reclaiming Conversation. The Power of Talk in a Digital Age.*

But something is missed, Turkie says, phones may also separate people. One dad reported his experience on a school field trip with his seven-year-old. He realized that while texting and sending photos to friends, he had ignored the opportunities to talk with his son. Another couple I know planned a cruise with their teenage sons, but the cruise was cancelled when the teenagers refused to go unless they had access to WiFi.

The nature of games on hand-held gadgets has become so mesmerizing that walking into traffic or a construction site is becoming a danger. Texting while driving carries even worse dangers.

Surfing.

The library and encyclopedia have been replaced for many students with a handheld that can search quickly through many sources. But while a trusted librarian can keep a student on track, a search engine can go in many directions, and the sources presented are not always friendly or in the best interests of the student. The trust a young student has in a discovered site may be greater than his trust of parents or teachers.

School Work.

Most schools now presume students have a computer device on hand and assignments often require some surfing. It's an opportunity for grandparents to stay up-to-date with their grandson or daughter's work.

2. Do They Have an Electronic Addiction?

Is addiction the right word here? Alcohol addictions were defined in **Suggestion 6** as persons whose drinking habits produce excessive absenteeism from work or school and complaints from friends and family.

How does an electronic addiction measure up to that definition? Excessive absenteeism could extend to times when your teen is at school but mentally absent because he is texting friends, surfing the web, or playing games. Complaints from family and friends would include times when a teenager is absorbed in his computer or mobile device and paying no attention to present company.

We already know alcohol-related car accidents will still be the biggest killer of our teens until they pass college age. Now we can add texting and multi-tasking to the reasons for the fatal crash.

3. The Dangers of Social Media.

Ninety-five percent of teens in the U.S. are online. Also, three out of four access the internet by cell phone or other mobile device.

Teenagers who fear being embarrassed often feel safe when tweeting, texting, or posting on Facebook. It allows more time to think over a potentially embarrassing faux pas, and it also allows them to be unidentified.

Nevertheless, it is also a danger to your teenager because unidentified people could be sending your offspring scams or worse. How old is the author of the next e-mail exchange with your grandson or daughter?

One father told me his son, who objected to his father invading his "online privacy," was arrested for distributing pornographic materials on the Net. His son had found some pictures of younger girls not quite dressed and in provocative positions. He sent them to "friends" on the Net one of whom was a detective posing as a teenager. His son was arrested. If charged and convicted, his record could follow him the rest of his life.

Keeping up-to-date on your teenager's internet activities could be a very important parental habit. Since we all know that anything online can be seen by anybody, this is not a privacy issue.

4. Friends, Bullies and Meanies All Chime In on the Net.

Bullies often prefer social media, because they not only have a victim but also an audience. Not just to admire them, but to add to the victim's embarrassment. Be an up-to-date companion when your grandson or daughter is on the Net.

"Let's look it up on google," your grandson may

say. Stay well informed with what your grandson or daughter is looking up on the Internet. Make a habit of asking them to show you what was interesting, frightening, or violent. Let your grandson have the computer seat while you watch, and the two of you talk over what is presented. Of course, you can't always watch, but as a frequent visitor, you will be more informed.

At some family times, the social media should be off-limits. For example, one person should not be staring into his or her lap at a little window at dinner time. The family table should be clear of these distractions.

Blocking some sites as off-limits can help, but how do you block the sites she or he will discover tomorrow?

Grandma: *"What are you doing on your cell phone?"*

Fifteen-year-old Marie: *"Just texting a...friend."*

Grandma: *"Who's the friend?"*

Marie: *"Grandma, do you have to know everything? Just a friend."*

Grandma: *"I just wondered."*

Marie: *"Don't I get any privacy? Do you need to know everything?"*

Grandma: *"No, but the Net is used by dangerous people. I don't want you to get into trouble."*

Marie: *"I'm doing my own private e-mails—it's nobody else's business."*

Grandma: *"Nothing is private on the Net. Anybody savvy enough to cut in can read your stuff."*

Marie: *"Oh, Grandma, nobody cares. I'm just talking to Jim somebody. He's not even in our school."*

Grandma: *"Wait, where does this friend live?"*

Marie: *"Grandma, I don't know. Around here somewhere, I guess. Leave me alone."*

Grandma: *"How old is he?"*

Marie: *"How should I know? Stay out of my private life."*

Grandma: *"This is on the Internet, so it's not your private life."*

Marie: *"What's the big deal? We met in this chat room I follow."*

Grandma: *"The big deal is you're talking to some boy (or man) you met in a chat room. You don't know his name, his age, or where he lives."*

Marie: *"Just bug out."*

Grandma: *"No, I can't bug out. You shouldn't e-mail this person again. And if he e-mails you, I *hope you will show it to me and your mother."*

Of course, this is not the end of this problem. Grandma needs to stay up-to-date on this conversation. If Marie remains cagey and secretive about "Jim Somebody," Grandma should be nosy until she's satisfied that Jim is a legitimate friend. Minors shouldn't have privacy on the public Internet, there are too many predators.

Marie needs to learn that social media is not private. There is a record of everything. This is not her diary. Online, it is always possible to keep records, and they can be reviewed for any purpose. Marie's access to the Net should remain limited until she is mature enough to be careful.

The most important part of managing a high-tech teenager is to be available--available to talk and listen to your grand-teen, to discuss his or her concerns, and to provide your adult perspective.

5. The Consequences of Being **Busted!**

Caught shoplifting or driving under the influence, very few children or teenagers, or even adults, would understand the circumstances, the lawyers, and a lot of other details you don't see in TV shows. Because of these vague aspects, your grand-teen might not have a clear understanding of the likely consequences for not-quite-innocent behavior. This lack of understanding can keep the deterrent aspect of our justice system from having its best effect on your grandchild-teenager.

Teens are likely to belittle a grandparent's warnings of consequences, and they may be partly right that they will get off easy the first time. So if short-term consequences are mild, emphasizing the long-term ones may sound pretty weak to the young and short-sighted.

At the moment of temptation, would a teen know a conviction for a drug-related Internet crime could exclude certain rights for the <u>rest of his life</u>? For example, he would never be able to get a private pilot's license for flying an airplane!

Unfortunately, many of the consequences require long-term thinking - not a familiar task for a teenager. The shadow of a conviction lasts a long time in these days of high-tech data banks. The system never really forgives you. Everyone gets to know, and your teen gets to keep few secrets. The information given on job, school, and loan applications is easily checked. You can't just "not tell them" anymore.

Grandparents should do their best to dispel the magical thinking and the self-serving delusions that are short on facts. Internet "friends" who may tempt your teen into trouble will always be short on facts.

For example, if your granddaughter or son were arrested for some Internet activity, would he or she know the possibility of waiting in jail? Would he know who is responsible for fines and expenses? How much do lawyers cost? Who has to pay?

In the long term, a conviction can also limit their future opportunities—job and credit applications will explore their record, and financial institutions will also. Will a conviction jeopardize a college loan or a job application at a computer programming company?

Teens need to know what they have to lose.

The Last Word: Graduation

Do you remember who attended your high school graduation? What about your grade school graduation?

You can't help but wonder if the graduate will even notice who's there with all the preparation and excitement of getting ready for graduation. But when you revisit your own memories, you realize you remember, and the attention and good wishes made a difference.

Whether you are the grandparent or just one of the extended family, you should go. Not so that years later they will remember you attended, as you remember who attended yours, but to provide the encouragement a child or teenager needs for the next step.

The kids may not thank you for the attention. They may not even recognize their own feelings about it. "Graduation? Don't worry about it" and "It's no big deal" are their usual reactions. But in their plans for celebration you can see that it is a big deal.

Even if it's "only grade school" or "only middle school," I would argue that your presence is even more important. How are your students to know their learning is being recognized if the important adults in their lives only show up for high school graduation? That's too late. The first graduations, preschool, elementary school, middle school, are events where your support can influence their efforts in later schooling.

I don't know how many parents, grandparents, grandmas, and uncles attended each student's grade school graduation. But if such statistics were available, I bet that on the average, their attendance at grade school and middle school graduations helped some students avoid dropping out before high school graduation.

Teens may feel obligated to give the impression that they are not interested in celebrations and congratulations. So it's tempting to relax your interest as the teens go through high school and beyond. But as the choices become more voluntary, you need to be even more supportive of what you know is the right direction.

The schools need the support also. Every teacher, principal, and political leader is aware, at least unconsciously, of attendance at school events. Make sure graduation keeps its priority over baseball and football in their minds. Your child's school, his next school, and your county system need to know you are concerned, and you expect fine schools and appreciate fine results.

It was only when my Grandma Manilla came to my way-out-of-town wedding that I brought it all together and realized that she had been at every milestone event of my life. Her presence had always been a part of my motivation for the next effort (I can't quit now, what will I tell Grandma Manilla?).

Kids are not likely to say, "Gee, I'm really glad you came." Your student is probably too distracted by all that is going on and not quite mature enough to recognize consciously how much it means. But later, as he or she feels the challenge of the next hurtle, the memory of your presence and encouragement may keep him or her going forward.

Here's where Woody Allen's remark is doubly true, "Eighty percent of life is just showing up."

www.ingramcontent.com/pod-product-compliance
Lightning Source LLC
Chambersburg PA
CBHW070604300426
44113CB00010B/1389